obscure

AUTHOR

JOEL LEGUNN teaches physics and mathematics in high school and junior high school. His laboratory courses tend to be innovative — stressing new experimental procedures that he devises with students. Mr. Legunn has worked as a science editor on *Physics Today,* a journal of the American Institute of Physics. He has written several science articles for young people and plans to continue writing and teaching.

CONSULTANTS FOR THIS BOOK

HARVEY POLLACK is an authority on multimedia education in physics, teaching machine technology, and computer systems for education. He has received 3 top awards from the National Science Teachers Association and is Senior Teacher of Physics at the Forest Hills High School in New York City. In addition to teaching and consulting, Mr. Pollack has written several books and more than 100 articles on physics and electronics.

ABRAM BADER has a distinguished career as a teacher of physics. He is Chairman of Physical Science at John Jay High School in New York City and has taught physics at 2 colleges. The American Association of Physics Teachers awarded Mr. Bader its citation for outstanding service. He continues to contribute to science education by teaching and such activities as serving on curricular and textbook committees.

GENE LIBERTY, Editor in Chief

A CREATIVE UNDERSTANDING BOOK

BY JOEL LEGUNN

MOTION

CREATIVE EDUCATION PRESS
Division of Creative Educational Society, Inc.
Mankato, Minnesota 56001

For my parents

●

ASSOCIATE EDITOR AND COVER ART: Jacolyn A. Mott
BOOK DESIGN: Harold Franklin / PHOTO RESEARCH: Jean Pedersen
ILLUSTRATIONS: Charles E. Peterson

●

Copyright © 1971 by Creative Educational Society, Inc.
International copyrights reserved in all countries — Printed in USA
No part of this book may be reproduced in any form, except for
reviews, without permission in writing from the publisher.

●

Library of Congress catalog card number 73-128852
Standard book number 87191-041-1

contents

	page
EDITOR'S NOTE: In favor of dreamers	4
chapter 1 WHAT IS MOTION?	5
2 THE MEASURE OF MOTION	14
3 FASTER AND FASTER AND . . .	24
4 PER SECOND PER SECOND	32
5 FORCE — THE MOVER	41
● SPECIAL SECTION: A picture gallery of motion	49
6 ENDLESS MOTION?	71
7 MOMENTUM	82
8 ROUND AND ROUND	98
● SPECIAL SECTION: Useful information	111
Oranges and apples — converting units	112
Table of motion conversions	114
Definitions	116
Recommended books and films	119
Index	121
Answers to problems	123
Acknowledgments	124

Editor's Note

IN FAVOR OF DREAMERS

Even during times when most men did not travel beyond their villages, men of imagination were thinking of ways to move off the Earth.

In 1638, the hero of a story by Francis Godwin flew to the Moon. His spacecraft — shown on our cover — was towed by trained swans. When he landed, he found a race of Moon people 28 feet tall.

The French poet and soldier Cyrano de Bergerac (1619-1655) wrote of his imaginary trip to the Moon on a firecracker chariot. Cyrano, too, found himself among Moon people. They put him in jail because of his wild claim that people were actually living on the planet Earth.

Cyrano was probably the first to predict that rocket flight would be necessary to go to the Moon. Godwin's astronaut found that he weighed less on the Moon and could jump greater distances than on Earth. It is startling to learn that this story was written some 50 years before Isaac Newton's brilliant work on the laws of gravity.

The great inventions of motion — wheels on land, hulls in water, and wings, rockets and jets in the air — have a history filled with far-out dreams.

Pause here and there in the book at an idea that particularly interests you. Then let the idea blow through your mind. Let it wind-lift your imagination like a balloon without a string that can go anywhere.

Science demands imagination. Even when we reject the impossible, our minds are stirred. Information is uncovered, and ideas are born. In fact, often we first need to ask, What is wrong? before we can discover what is true.

Gene Liberty

Chapter 1
WHAT IS MOTION?

Your home rests firmly on the Earth — motionless. It has remained in the same place since it was built. Your bed is stationary on the floor of your quiet room. The time is night. You are about to fall asleep, and you feel as peaceful as your surroundings. Everything is at rest. Or is it?

Motion inside you

While you lie still, your lungs move continuously. Expanding and contracting, they pull in fresh air and push out used air that contains carbon dioxide. Pumping rhythmically, your heart moves all the blood in your body through its chambers about every minute and a half. The blood, always in motion, streams through some 60,000 miles of blood vessels.

The cells in your body take oxygen from your blood and give up carbon dioxide in exchange. Each cell is made up of billions of atoms and molecules that *vibrate*

STARRY NIGHT
Is the world at night a quiet place? Not according to the artist Vincent Van Gogh, who painted the skies and the Earth swirling with motion.

RANDOM MOTION
The dot represents a molecule of gas. The lines and the arrow suggest the unpredictable path the molecule travels in the air. Such motion is called Brownian movement.

(move back and forth) endlessly. Countless electrons spin and whirl inside these atoms and molecules about a million billion times per second. Yet you have hardly moved.

Leaping molecules

Everywhere in your room, motion continues without interruption. The walls, floor, ceiling, and all the furniture contain atoms and molecules that swirl, shake, spin, and vibrate. Molecules of air, racing at random (in all directions), collide and transfer some of their motion to each other. Turn on a flashlight in a darkened room. You will see how the dust particles in the air are kicked in all directions by moving air molecules.

If you keep a glass of water in your room, you will notice that some of the water disappears overnight. Water molecules take part in that same whirling dance that goes on in air. Some of the water molecules leap from the surface and vaporize into the air.

Outside your house, in the deceptive stillness of the night, movement never ceases. Surrounding the Earth, an ocean of air that weighs 5,600 million million tons churns with excited motion. Even on the quietest night, when no breeze stirs, every particle of air jumps about and strikes other particles. This ceaseless turmoil helps to produce gentle breezes, powerful hurricanes, whirling tornadoes, and all the other events that we call weather.

CAN YOU HEAR MOTION?
Yes — sound waves are made up of air molecules that vibrate (move back and forth). In this photograph, sound waves create motion in a liquid.

BUILDING BLOCKS
All matter is made up of extremely small particles called atoms — the building blocks of the universe. When atoms group together to build a substance, they form molecules.

In the photograph, each ball represents an atom. The rods join atoms to make models of molecules.

END OF A TRIP
The vegetation on isolated islands such as these in the Pacific is often started by seeds carried in by winds and waves. Some of the plants seen here may have relatives thousands of miles away.

Each day, billions of gallons of water evaporate from the oceans and other bodies of water. This water, in the form of vapor, rises and forms clouds that may drift for thousands of miles before it falls to Earth as rain, snow, sleet, or hail.

Journeys — long and short

Seeds and pollen that ride on invisible currents of air fall to Earth, sometimes many miles from their mother plants, to start new life in distant places.

While you sleep, other forms of life may be in the midst of great journeys. Birds such as the golden plover may be winging nonstop across thousands of miles of ocean, en route from northern Canada to the Hawaiian Islands. Perhaps the green turtle is on its extended pilgrimage from the coast of Brazil, where it feeds, to Ascension Island, in the South Atlantic, where it lays eggs — a distance of 1,400 miles. At the bottom of the world, the Adelie penguin may be traveling hundreds of miles on its semiannual (twice yearly) migration over the polar ice cap.

All around you in ponds, lakes, and rivers — even in a muddy puddle of water — many invisible 1-celled creatures dart about in search of food. Examine just 1 drop of this water with a microscope. You may see hundreds of oval-shaped paramecia paddling about with little oar-like hairs, called cilia. Or perhaps you will find amoebae

7

HITCHHIKERS IN THE AIR
These red maple seed pods will ride the wind, and where their journeys end, new plants will grow. Pollen are also carried by the wind and by birds, insects, and other animals.

QUIET POND?
Below the surface of these still waters, microorganisms are in motion everywhere. Through a microscope (circle), they can be observed moving in all directions. Their activity, along with the random motion of water molecules, make this a not-so-quiet pond.

pulling themselves along by means of pseudopods (false feet), as they try to engulf bits of food.

If all this is not enough, think of that restless animal — man. During every minute of the day and night, cars, trains, ships, and planes are rolling, steaming, and jetting around the globe. They transport people in every possible direction to a multitude of different destinations. And no matter what the time, someone somewhere is climbing a stairway or walking on a street.

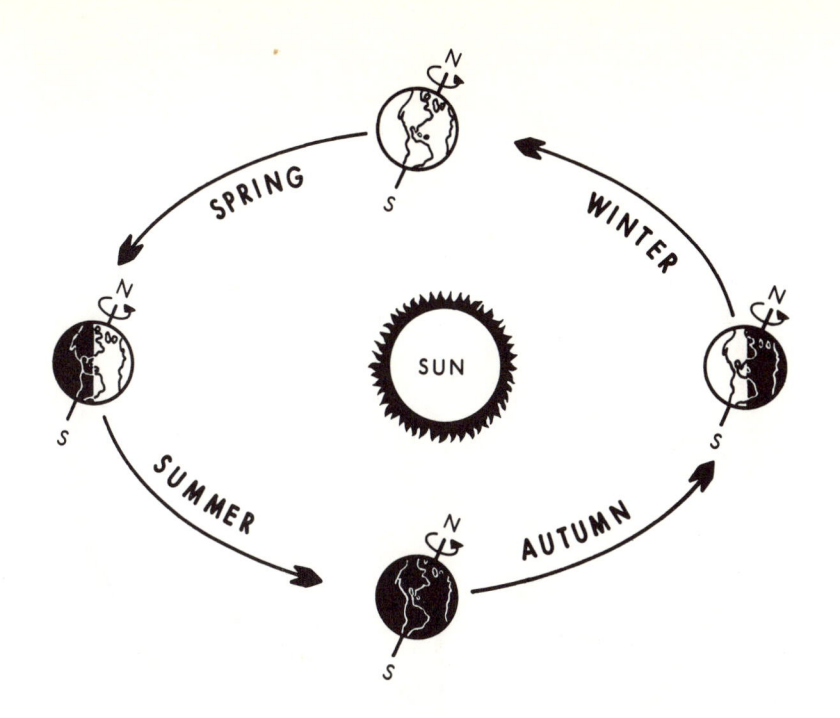

A YEAR'S JOURNEY
The Earth follows the path of an ellipse as it revolves around the Sun. It takes 1 year to make a full trip: 365 days, 5 hours, 48 minutes, and 46 seconds. During this trip of almost 600 million miles, the changing angle of the Sun's rays creates the 4 seasons.

Nothing is still

Surely there must be something at rest.

Is it your bed? The Earth, on which your house stands, is rotating like a spinning top. If you live at the Equator, your house travels in a circle at about 1,000 miles per hour. The Earth is also revolving around the Sun. On this yearly trip, the Earth hurtles through space at 66,000 miles per hour, almost four times faster than an orbiting artificial satellite.

The Sun and all the heavenly bodies that travel around it, such as the 9 planets, the moons, and the comets, are called the *solar system*. Although we think of the solar system as gigantic, it is nothing more than a few dots in a larger system — the galaxy known as the Milky Way. The solar system itself is not at rest. It revolves around the center of the Milky Way at 482,000 miles per hour.

From the tiniest amoeba to the biggest star, everything in the universe is in constant motion.

Let us ask again: Is there anything that has no motion? The answer is no. Then can we ever say that anything is at rest? Yes, we can. Apparently we have a contradiction. If everything has motion, how can anything be thought of as being at rest?

ROTATING SLEEPER

While this man sleeps and sleeps, the Earth rotates. If you were on a stationary satellite high above the North Pole, you would observe him traveling on a circular path thousands of miles long. How long has he been asleep when he passes point A?

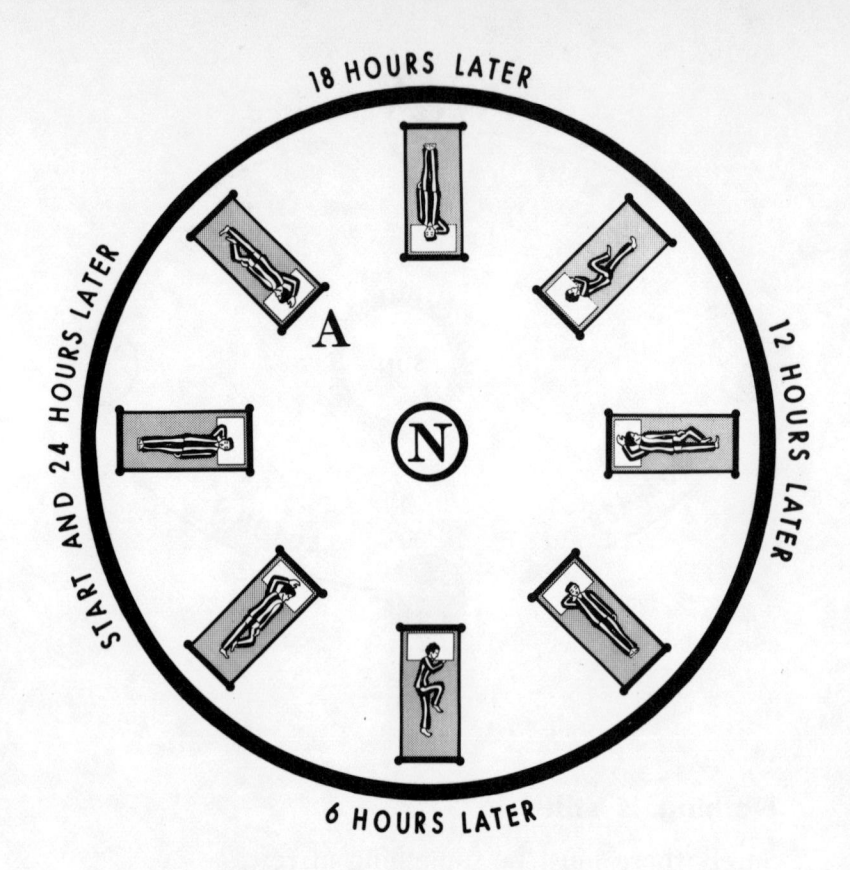

Strangely, both can be right

We said you are at rest in your bed. What do we mean? If someone looks into your room, he will see you in the same place in your bed, which occupies the same place on the floor. He would say you are at rest. Suppose that a second person on a space platform 100 miles above the North Pole could also see you. He would observe that you are moving in a circle (because of the rotation of the Earth). According to his testimony, you are in motion. Who is right?

Strangely enough, both observers are right. The first describes your motion with reference to your room. The second describes your motion with reference to the space platform.

Downstairs or upstairs?

We describe the motion or position of an object by referring to a specific location, called a *frame of reference*.

Because the 2 observers occupy different frames of reference, one sees your motion; the other does not. After a frame of reference is agreed on, however, there is generally no dispute about an object's position or motion.

Suppose that your house has 3 floors and that your room is on the second floor. A friend standing outside your house sees your father at a window on the third floor. He asks where you are. Your father answers that you are *downstairs* in your room.

At the same time, another friend telephones. When your mother answers the phone in the kitchen, which is on the first floor, she says that you are *upstairs* in your room.

Both your mother and father are referring to the same room, but each describes its location from a different frame of reference. Of course, they both may say that you are in your room on the *second floor*. In that case, the frame of reference of both your parents is the whole house — rather than their own locations.

A traveler's predicament

Imagine, if you will, that you have just boarded a very special train. Of ultra-modern design, this train runs so smoothly that it makes no noise, nor does it shake from side to side as it moves. It is night; the shades have been drawn, and you fall asleep.

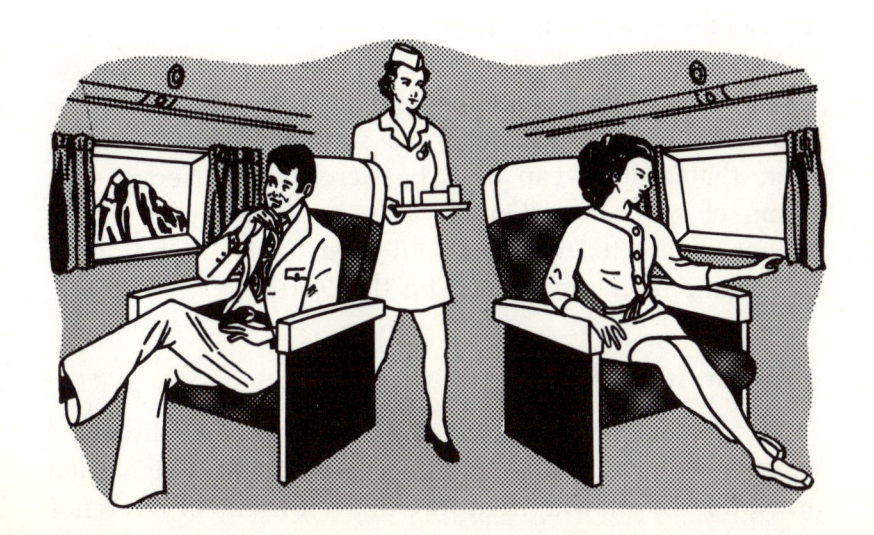

WHICH WAY IS UP?
Imagine that you are standing at the North Pole and throw a ball up into the air. Another person at the South Pole also throws a ball up into the air. Your "up" and his "up" are in opposite directions. "Up and "down" only have the same meaning to people in the same frame of reference.

SEEING MOTION
The passenger on the right sees nothing when she looks out of the airplane window. Thus she cannot tell that she is in motion. But the passenger on the left observes that the airplane is passing a mountain. Because of this reference, he can tell that he is moving.

UP OR DOWN — HOW CAN YOU TELL?
The walls of this windowless elevator hide all outside frames of reference. If the elevator moves very smoothly, the passengers will not know whether they are riding up, down, or standing still.

AM I MOVING?
Inside this ship in deep space, the astronaut cannot tell that he is moving even if he looks out the window. Although the stars are visible, they are too far away to serve as a frame of reference for motion.

A short time later, you awaken and wonder if the train is on its journey. Because the train runs so smoothly, you cannot tell whether or not you are in motion. To find out if you are actually moving, you raise the shade on 1 side of the train and see that you are whizzing past another train. Or is it whizzing past you in the opposite direction?

If you raise the shade on the other side of the train, you can find out. Surprisingly, you see that you have not yet left the station. It is the other train that is moving.

It seemed that your train was in motion relative (when compared) to the other train. But relative to the station and the Earth, you have not moved. Again, observations from different frames of reference result in different descriptions of the same event.

The most common reference

One condition seems to be necessary every time we observe motion: A frame of reference is always required to describe the position or motion of objects. There is no motion, in fact, without regard to some frame of reference.

The most common frame of reference for all of us is the Earth. Although the Earth spins like a top and also moves around the Sun, we conveniently consider it to be stationary. We measure our motion along the Earth's surface as we move from place to place on it. We can, for instance, take as a frame of reference a well-known landmark, a street, or even a whole town, all of which are fixed rigidly to the Earth.

Although we will discuss the position and motion of objects many times, we may not always specify a particular frame of reference. We should remember, however, that motion can only be described in terms of a frame of reference. One is always present even if we do not choose to identify it. In most cases, the unidentified frame of reference will be the Earth.

What is motion?

So far, we have talked about motion and discussed where and how it takes place. We even put a limitation on motion by showing that it requires a frame of reference to be described. But we have not defined it. In order to

EVERYDAY POINTS OF REFERENCE

Outstanding parts of our environment serve as reference points for travelers. For example, monuments, tall buildings, and unusual earth formations are convenient places to meet and to check distances and directions.

study motion more completely, we should agree on its meaning.

Everyday experience tells us that an object in motion can go faster, slow down, or continue at the same speed. To define motion, we can combine this experience with the knowledge that a moving object must be described in a frame of reference:

Motion is a continuous change of position.

A moving object, therefore, can change its position quickly or slowly — but it cannot remain in the same position. If it does, it is said to be at rest. These, then, are 2 opposite conditions — rest and motion. Between them is a science that is fascinating, perhaps because it does not just belong in a laboratory but is so much a part of everything we do and see.

MOTION PICTURES

Why do these pictures agree with our definition of motion? It is natural to assume that the car is riding past the house. But imagine that the house is moving past the car. Do the pictures still agree with the definition?

13

Chapter 2
THE MEASURE OF MOTION

When you walk to a friend's home, you do not usually measure how fast you are moving or calculate the distance that you travel. Instead, you rely on experience to estimate the time for your trip. Frequently, however, it is not practical to depend on such rough estimates. A more accurate measure of motion is needed.

This accuracy is based on certain measurements that are helpful in describing motion, like distance and time. From these, we can develop other measurements, such as speed, velocity, and acceleration. All of these terms have a familiar sound because they are commonly used. However, our everyday understanding of them may be different from that of scientists. It will be helpful to sharpen our definitions to match theirs.

From start to finish

Fortunately, the ordinary meaning of time — How long did it take? — does not have to be altered for the study of motion. For example, a baseball leaves a pitcher's hand and arrives at a catcher's mitt after a certain length of time. Here, *time* measures the interval between 2 given events: the beginning and the end of an action.

In order to measure time, we need a common standard

NO MORE FUEL!
That was the problem the gallant adventurer Phileas Fogg had to solve on the last part of his journey in the book *Around the World in 80 Days*.

Fogg was crossing the Atlantic by steamship. When fuel ran short, he had his men burn every piece of wood they could pull off the ship. Bunks, cabins, railings, even the figurehead (picture) were sacrificed to successfully bring them to port.

TIME OF A PITCH
This interval starts for the batter the instant the ball leaves the pitcher's hand (arrow). It ends when the batter either hits the ball or strikes.

EARTH VIEW OF THE STARS
As seen from the North Pole, the stars seem to sweep out circular tracks. At the Equator, they seem to move in straight bands. The rotation of the Earth — carrying the camera with it — creates these patterns.

The lens of the camera is left open to capture the continuous motion. What is the shortest time the camera could have been open at the North Pole? The answer appears at the end of the index.

that will let us know how much of it passes during any action. We have this standard — the second. Based on the rotation (turning) of the Earth, the second is the accepted unit of time throughout the world. The rotation of the Earth is almost constant — that is, it changes very little over the centuries. The result is a day of practically constant length.

The day is divided into 24 hours. Each hour is divided into 60 minutes and each minute into 60 seconds. There are 60×60, or 3,600, seconds in an hour. A day contains $24 \times 3,600$, or 86,400 seconds. One second can therefore be considered as 1/86,400 of a day.

Location does not matter

To measure the length of an interval, we note the starting time and finishing time of an action. Two different clocks measuring the same action need not have the same starting and finishing times. But they must tick off standard seconds accurately in order to measure the same interval, for example:

The interval of a jet flight from San Francisco to New York can be measured with clocks at each location. But there is a 3-hour difference between New York time and San Francisco time. Suppose that the flight starts at 1:00 PM San Francisco time. A radio signal is sent to New York at take-off time. It is 4:00 PM in New York.

The jet lands in New York at 9:00 PM. A radio signal is immediately sent from New York to San Francisco. The

15

signal is received at 6:00 PM in San Francisco.

The starting and finishing times are different in the 2 locations. In San Francisco, they are 1:00 PM and 6:00 PM; and in New York, they are 4:00 PM and 9:00 PM. Both clocks, however, tick off seconds of equal length, and both measure the same interval — 5 hours.

Two kinds of distances

Motion occurs in space as well as in time. But distance — the measurement of space — often is not what it appears to be. Let us see why.

Imagine that 3 teachers have to fly to another city to attend a meeting. Each drives from the school to the airport by a different route. The first teacher likes scenery and takes a route shaped like a triangle. The second teacher takes a straight route because he starts out late and is anxious to reach the airport quickly. The third teacher has to stop and pick up a passenger. He goes out of his way and takes a route that follows a rectangular path.

All 3 teachers reach the same destination, the airport. "What is the distance from the school to the airport?" we wonder. If we check the mileage gauges on the 3 automobiles, we will get 3 different answers. Which is correct? To answer the question, we have to recognize that there are 2 kinds of distances. One is total path, the other displacement.

Actual or shortest?

Total path is the actual distance traveled by a moving object, including all curves and turns that may be present. We can compare the total paths traveled by the 3 teachers on the map. Route 3 is the longest total path; Route 2 is the shortest; and Route 1 is in between.

The shortest total path between 2 points — Route 2 in this example — is always a straight line. Route 2 has a certain length (found by measuring along a straight line), and the car on it travels in 1 direction.

Distance along a straight line in 1 direction is known as *displacement*. In the study of motion, when we speak of distance we mean total path rather than displacement. Of course, at times — as with Route 2 — they are the same.

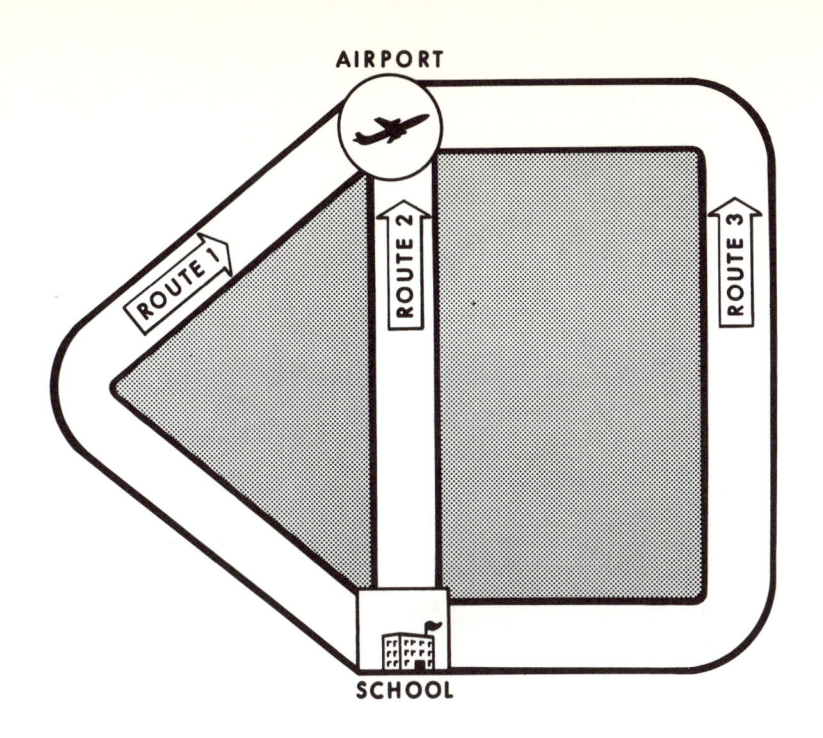

ALTERNATE ROUTES

This map shows the different routes taken by the 3 teachers to reach the airport from the school. The distance each travels is different, but their displacements are the same.

AS THE CROW FLIES

On this map, 1 inch equals 1 mile. What is the displacement of each? How many more miles did the man travel than the bird? Use a ruler to find the answers. Check them against those given at the end of the index.

The man walks a winding route (dark dotted line) to reach his destination. The bird flies straight to the same destination (open dotted line).

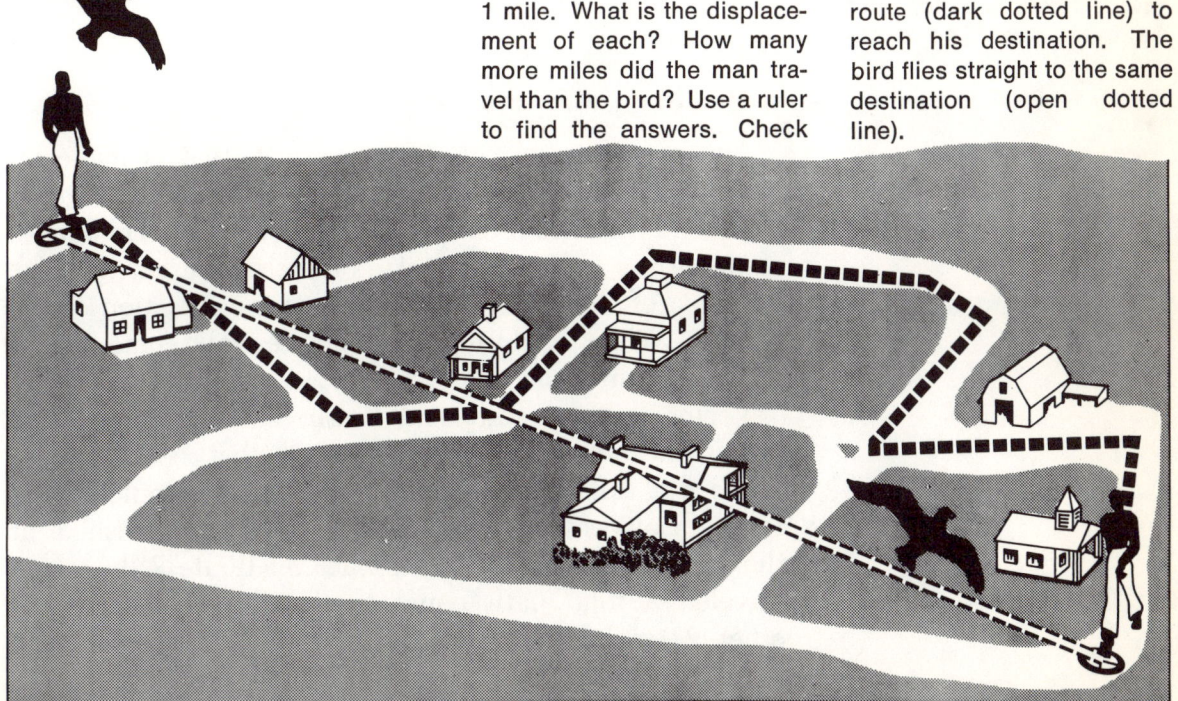

17

1 MILE
EAST

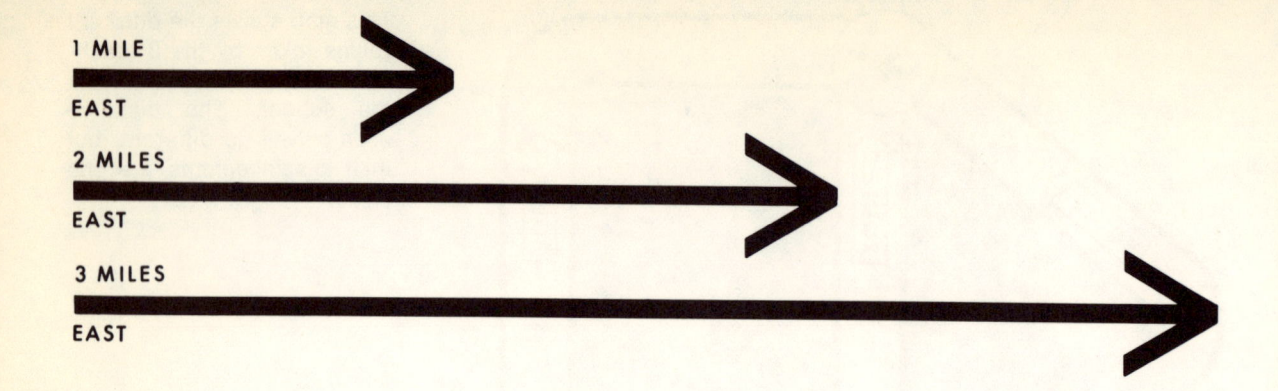

2 MILES
EAST

3 MILES
EAST

VECTORS

These lines are vectors that represent displacement — distance along a straight line in 1 direction.

The lines at the top show that displacements can have the same direction but different sizes. The lengths of the lines show the size of the displacements. For example, the 2-mile line is twice as big as the 1-mile line.

The lines at the bottom show that displacements can have different directions but the same size. The direction of a vector is usually shown, as here, with arrowheads.

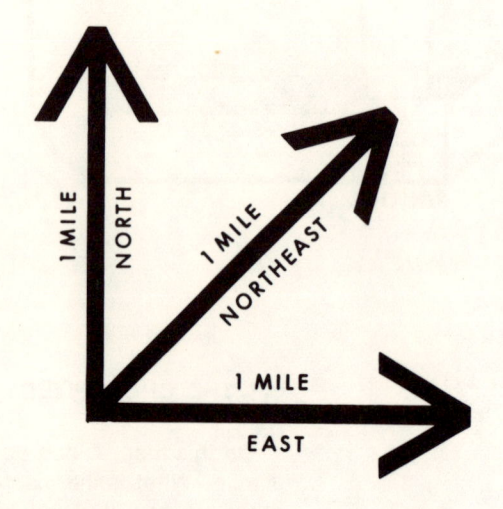

1 MILE NORTH
1 MILE NORTHEAST
1 MILE EAST

Vectors point the way

Any measurement, like displacement, that is made up of both direction and size or amount is called a *vector*. Frequently vectors are represented by arrows. The length of the arrow indicates the size of the measurement. The direction of the arrow is the same as the direction of the vector. While exploring motion, we will come across many measurements that are vectors.

Vectors have a start and finish, like the school and airport in our example. We noted that each teacher traveled a different total path. But all 3 completed the same displacement since they started and finished at the same points. Only the teacher on Route 2, however, traveled a total path equal to the displacement. The other 2 teachers traveled paths that were greater than the displacement.

Displacement, therefore, can be equal to or less than the total path covered. In fact, it can be zero. If you run completely around a circular track, your displacement is zero. Your total path, however, equals the length of the track. (The length of, or distance around, a circle is called the *circumference*.)

What direction?

To see why direction is as important as distance, suppose we look further into displacement. Imagine that a ranger, on a recovery mission, has just bailed out of a plane onto a desert. According to the pilot, the ranger will land at a spot 10 miles from the nearest town. After the ranger picks up a piece of lost equipment at that spot in the desert, he must reach the town.

If the ranger walks in a straight line for 10 miles, he still may not reach town. Why? He must know what direction to follow. He takes a compass and map out of his knapsack and learns that he must head north. Now the ranger knows both the distance and the direction he must travel, and he starts out confidently.

Speed

Two other aspects of the ranger's hike to town interest us: How long did it take him to walk the 10 miles? Was his direction always true north?

When we want to know how fast or slow anything moves, we measure its *speed* — the total path a moving object travels per unit of time. Let us break this definition down to make sure we understand its parts. *Total*

ZERO DISPLACEMENT
The boomerang soars into the air and returns to the thrower. Although the total path (actual distance) it travels is long, the displacement is zero. Why?

FINDING THE WAY
A wanderer in the desert can find his direction by stars, landmarks, and the sun. However, if he does not count or time his steps, he cannot know the distance he walks.

path, as we have said, means *distance* traveled in any direction. *Per*, in the language of science, means *divided by* or *each*. A *unit of time* is a single measurement of time, like 1 second, 1 minute, or 1 hour.

Speed, therefore, equals distance divided by time, which can be written

$$\text{speed} = \frac{\text{distance}}{\text{time}}, \text{ or distance/time}$$

It is often convenient to write this formula as

$$\text{distance} = \text{speed} \times \text{time}$$

(A *formula* is a mathematical statement that shows how different quantities are related to one another.)

We stated that the ranger landed 10 miles from town. On his hike back, he wandered off compass and walked 12 miles over a period of 6 hours. What was his speed? Speed = distance/time = 12 miles/6 hours = 2 miles/hour. We can write 2 miles/hour several other ways:

$$2 \text{ mi/hr}, \ 2\frac{\text{miles}}{\text{hour}}, \ 2\frac{\text{mi}}{\text{hr}}, \ 2 \text{ miles per hour, and } 2 \text{ mph}$$

Distance (total path) can be measured in any unit of length. For example, instead of miles we can choose feet, inches, or yards. The same is true for time. Hours, minutes, and seconds are equally available. Thus speed can be expressed in many ways, including miles per minute, ft/sec, ft/min, and inches per hour.

After 1 second . . . 2 . . . 3 . . .

Suppose we look at what happens when an object moves at a speed of 10 ft/sec. Another way of describing this speed is to say that the object changes position at the rate of 10 ft/sec. It starts from rest, or zero speed. After 1 second, it has traveled a distance of 10 feet. At the end of 2 seconds, it has traveled another 10 feet. When the third second is up, it has traveled still another 10 feet. The distance it has traveled after 3 seconds equals 30 feet.

This kind of step-by-step reasoning is often valuable in science. In this instance, it helps develop an understanding of how distance, speed, and time are related to each other. The same reasoning applies, of course, to any speed expressed in any way, for example, 100 yards/sec, 60 mi/hr, or 50 centimeters/minute (1 centimeter equals 2.54 inches).

However, when we know an object's speed, there is a simpler way to find the distance it travels. We can apply the expression distance = speed × time. For instance, let us find the distance traveled by a car moving steadily at 100 ft/sec after 12 seconds.

$$\text{distance} = \text{speed} \times \text{time}$$
$$= 100 \, \frac{\text{ft}}{\text{sec}} \times 12 \, \text{sec}$$
$$= 1{,}200 \, \text{ft}$$

Comparing speeds

What about an object that moves very slowly, like a snail? "A snail's pace" is about 2 feet per hour. How far can a snail travel in 1 day (24 hours)?

SPEED
Each second after she begins walking, the girl increases the distance from her starting point by another 3 feet. Speed equals distance divided by time. What is her speed after 1 second? After 3 seconds? The answers appear at the end of the index.

21

SLOW MOTION

Speed often is the key to staying alive in the animal world. But slow as it is, the snail generally manages to find its food and evade its enemies.

Suppose the snail in the picture started crawling around this page when you began reading this book. In the time that you have been reading, the snail would have advanced only about halfway around the page.

$$\begin{aligned} \text{distance} &= \text{speed} \times \text{time} \\ &= 2\,\frac{\text{ft}}{\text{hr}} \times 24\,\text{hr} \\ &= 48\,\text{ft} \end{aligned}$$

Now let us find out how long it takes a snail to travel 1 mile. Can you guess — a week, a month, a year? Simple arithmetic will provide the answer. There are 5,280 feet in 1 mile. Since the snail travels 48 feet in 1 day, it will take 5,280 ft/mi ÷ 48 ft/day, or 110 days, to cover a distance of 1 mile. It is a good thing that the snail carries his shell-house with him. Otherwise after a 1-mile trip he would never find it again.

How do the speeds of the ranger, the car, and the snail compare?

ranger: 2 mi/hr

car: 100 ft/sec

snail: 2 ft/hr

It is difficult to check these figures against one another because they are not in the same speed units. For example, we cannot quickly see whether 100 ft/sec is faster or slower than 2 mi/hr.

One convenient approach to this problem is to make all speed units the same, say, mi/hr. In effect, we will place the 3 moving objects in the same race. We will measure the distances they travel with the same ruler and their times of travel with the same clock.

To learn more about how 1 unit of measurement can be changed into another, see pages 112–115.

22

True for all moving objects

Starting with the car, we will change ft/sec into ft/hr and then into mi/hr. Sound hard? It really is not. There are 3,600 seconds in an hour. Therefore, 100 ft/sec × 3,600 sec/hr = 360,000 ft/hr. We have already noted that 5,280 ft = 1 mi. To change ft/hr into mi/hr, we divide 360,000 ft/hr by 5,280 ft/mi and obtain 68 mi/hr.

Similarly, we will change the snail's speed from ft/hr into mi/hr. This time, the bottom parts of the fractions are the same. We only have to go through 1 step — changing the top parts. To change ft/hr into mi/hr, we divide 2 ft/hr by 5,280 ft/mi and obtain 1/2640th of a mile per hour, or .0004 mi/hr.

Now we can again compare the speeds of the ranger, the car, and the snail:

ranger: 2 mi/hr

car: 68 mi/hr

snail: 1/2640 mi/hr, or .0004 mi/hr

These 3 speeds are very different. For instance, the car is 68/2, or 34, times faster than the ranger. It is also 68/.004, or 17,000, times faster than the snail. Yet, as we saw, the same relationship — distance = speed × time — applies to the 3 moving objects. We can consider this relationship to be true for all moving objects, fast or slow.

CHAMPION RUNNER
Known as the fastest land animal, the cheetah can streak along at the incredible speed of 70 miles/hour. By comparison, the fastest human has run the mile in 3 minutes, 51.1 seconds — about 15.5 miles/hour.

Chapter 3
FASTER AND FASTER AND...

Man has long been dissatisfied with his inability to move quickly. He has built machines — especially during the past 150 years — that carry him faster than any other creature on the ground or in the sky. Each new generation of machines usually travels at higher speeds than its ancestors. As the "generation gap" between machines grows, so does the speed gap.

25 mi/hr to 25,000 mi/hr

In the early 1900s, automobiles were beginning to put-put their way — at speeds of about 25 mi/hr — into the American public's favor. If drivers then could have looked more than half a century into the future, few would have believed that the *Spirit of America — Sonic I* was a descendant of their own vehicles. On November 15, 1965, Craig Breedlove, a racing driver, stepped into the jet-propelled *Spirit*. Minutes after he ignited its jets, the *Spirit* was racing along at 601.1 mi/hr — the fastest speed ever attained by a 4-wheel automobile.

Airplanes began to develop at about the same time as automobiles. The Wright brothers first tested their new engine-driven airplane on December 17, 1903. They took off and landed on a desolate beach at the village of Kitty

FAST AS A PLANE
This jet-powered car has reached speeds comparable to those of modern aircraft — 601.1 miles/hour. At such speeds, a bump in the road could send the car wildly off course. For this reason, it is driven on the smooth Bonneville Salt Flats in Utah.

EARLY RACER
The "buggyaut" was the first automobile sold to the public in the United States. It was built by the Duryea brothers between 1893 and 1894. One year later a Duryea buggyaut proved its worth by outracing heavier, more expensive imported cars.

Hawk on the North Carolina coast. During their short hops — the longest was 852 feet — they flew at speeds of 7 to 10 mi/hr. Today's jet planes streak through the air at speeds of about 600 mi/hr. Farther away from Earth's atmosphere, astronauts have reached speeds of about 25,000 mi/hr.

Importance of direction

The speed of a moving object, whether it be a racing car or a turtle, only tells us how fast its position changes. We should also know its direction of travel, which is determined by a straight line. Recall, too, that distance along a straight line in 1 direction is known as *displacement*.

We now have a natural combination — speed and displacement. This combination, called *velocity*, means speed in a given direction. Velocity can also be expressed as the displacement of a moving object per unit of time.

Both velocity and speed measure how fast an object changes position. In everyday language, these terms often are given the same meaning. But in science, an all-important difference exists: Velocity has direction, and speed does not. As a scientist observed, "Velocity is speed that knows where it is going."

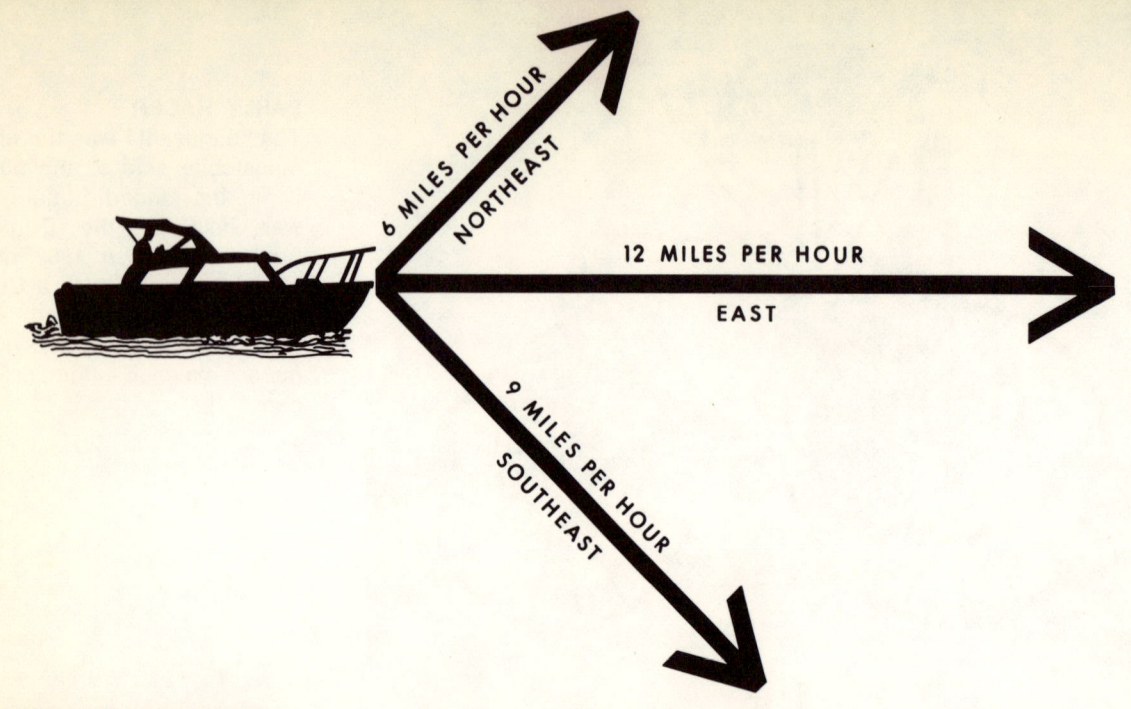

SPEED AND DIRECTION

Velocity is speed in a given direction. The upper vector represents the velocity of the wind. The lower vector represents the velocity of the water current.

Thus the boat is being pushed by natural forces in 2 directions — northeast and southeast. To move in a third direction — east (middle vector) — the boat's engine must create a push powerful enough to overcome the wind and the current.

Velocity is a vector

We defined speed as being equal to distance divided by time. That is, speed = distance/time. If we express velocity in a similar way, we see that

$$\text{velocity} = \frac{\text{displacement}}{\text{time}}$$

This formula can also be written as

$$\text{displacement} = \text{velocity} \times \text{time}$$

When describing the velocity of a moving object, we state both its speed and its direction — for example, 20 mi/hr, north. In chapter 2, we stated that any measurement that has both size or amount (20 mi/hr) and direction (north) is a *vector*. Velocity, therefore, is a vector.

Whirling cups for speed

One vector that affects and interests all of us is wind velocity. Two instruments are used in weather stations all over the world to measure wind motion — the anemometer and the weather vane. Usually these instruments are mounted on the roof of the weather station.

The cup anemometer, a common type, has 3 or 4 open cups mounted on horizontal arms (see photograph). Each arm is connected to a central shaft that turns. When the wind blows, it pushes the cups, forcing them to move. A light breeze turns the cups slowly, but a strong wind whirls them around rapidly. The center shaft, which is turned by the cups, is connected to a speedometer inside the building.

The weather vane also is mounted on a shaft that turns freely. The flat sail of the weather vane is pushed by the wind, so that the opposite, small end points into the wind. On weather vanes that are mounted on homes, the small end often is shaped like an arrow. If we speak of a west wind, we mean a wind that comes from the west. That is the direction towards which the small end (or point of the arrow) will face.

On a winding road

When we compared displacement with total path (distance), we observed:

▶ They both may be equal (motion along a straight path).

MEASURING THE WIND
The anemometer (cups) shows wind speed. The weather vane (flat sail) shows wind direction. By combining speed and direction, the weatherman obtains the vector measurement of wind motion — velocity.

DISTANCE VS. DISPLACEMENT
The runners circle the track several times, covering a considerable distance. Their displacements, however, equal zero because they start and finish at the same place.

▶ Displacement may be zero even though distance is not (motion around a circular path with the same starting and finishing point).

▶ Distance may be larger than displacement (motion along a winding path).

As we might expect, velocity and speed also can be compared in some ways:

▶ They both may be equal in size (motion along a straight path).

▶ Speed may be larger than the size of velocity (motion along a winding path). For example, suppose that a car is traveling on a winding road between 2 towns. A straight-line distance of 10 miles separates the towns. The trip takes 1 hour. Upon arriving at the second town, the driver reads the mileage gauge and learns that he has traveled 15 miles.

He correctly concludes that the car's speed was 15 mi/hr. But the car's displacement was 10 miles. Its velocity, therefore, was 10 mi/hr in the direction of the vector — the straight line connecting the towns.

Size without direction

Although velocity is a vector measurement, speed is not. Any measurement of size without direction, like speed, is called a *scalar*. Time, too, is a scalar. It describes the size of an interval but does not have any direction. Is temperature a vector? Is weight a scalar? The answers appear at the end of the index.

A scalar changes when its size changes — for example, a speed of 100 mi/hr that drops to 80 mi/hr or rises to 150 mi/hr. A vector, however, changes when its size or its direction changes. Consider a runner on a circular track who moves at constant speed. His direction continuously changes — and, therefore, his velocity continuously changes.

Imagine that the runner is now on a straight track. His direction is constant. If he continues to move at constant speed, his velocity will remain the same. But if his speed changes, his velocity will, too.

SIZE
WITHOUT DIRECTION

These instruments measure scalar quantities. Temperature is measured in degrees; time in hours, minutes, and seconds; length in inches; steam pressure in pounds per square inch; and barometric pressure in inches of mercury.

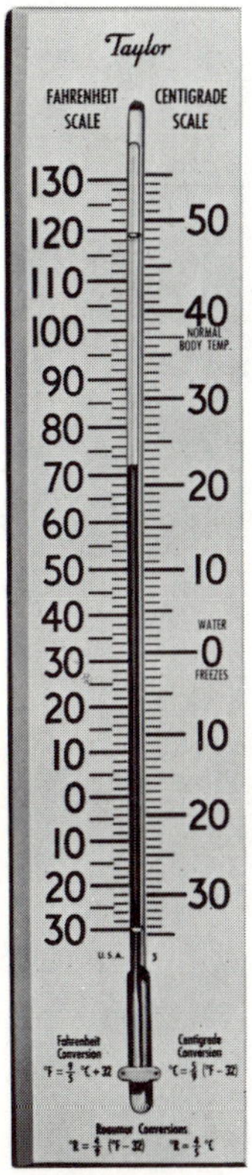

Thermometer

Clock

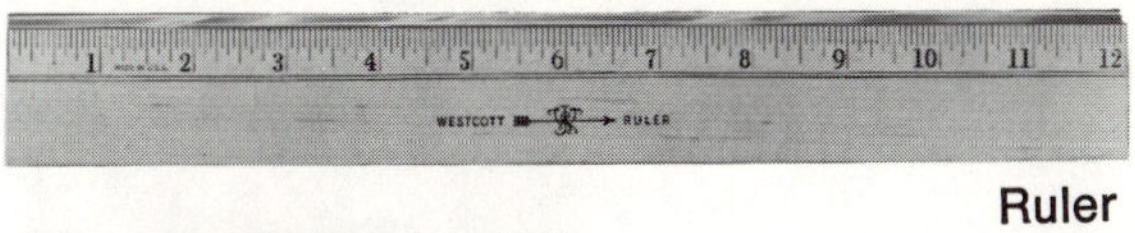

Ruler

Steam gauge

Barometer

When speed or direction changes

Most of the time in the world around us, velocity is not truly constant. If the runner sprints 100 yards south in 10 seconds on a straight track, his

$$\text{velocity} = \frac{\text{displacement}}{\text{time}}$$

$$= \frac{100 \text{ yards, south}}{10 \text{ seconds}}$$

$$= \frac{10 \text{ yd}}{\text{sec}}, \text{ south}$$

ZERO VELOCITY, THEN... The rocket accelerates after the fuel is ignited because it changes its velocity. It moves from zero velocity (rest) to a high velocity in seconds.

At different times during the sprint, the runner actually may be traveling slower or faster than 10 yd/sec, south. Thus 10 yd/sec, south is really an *average velocity*.

It is sometimes helpful in solving problems to treat an average velocity as if it were a *constant velocity* — 1 speed in 1 direction. However, when a change in velocity does occur, it produces an acceleration. This measurement is often necessary in the study of motion. A moving body accelerates when either its speed or its direction changes. *Acceleration* equals change in velocity divided by time, which can be written

$$\text{acceleration} = \frac{\text{change in velocity}}{\text{time}}$$

This formula also tells us that the velocity of an accelerating object equals its acceleration multiplied by the amount of time it has been accelerating.

$$\text{velocity} = \text{acceleration} \times \text{time}$$

Choice of suitable units

We have been expressing velocity in units of length divided by time, for example, feet/second, or feet per second. Recall that *per* means *divided by*. In what units is acceleration expressed? Acceleration = velocity/time. Its units, therefore, are feet/second divided by seconds, $\frac{\text{feet/second}}{\text{second}}$, or feet per second per second, or feet per second in each second.

Note: In this example, we are using feet for length and seconds for time. However, we can use inches and hours or any other units that are suitable.

If the units that express acceleration — like feet per second per second — are unfamiliar, they may seem puzzling. However, all that the 2 *pers* require is 2 divisions. The reason why can be readily understood by examining a simple accelerated motion, like walking faster and faster. This is something you will be asked to do — at least in your mind — in the next chapter. Per second per second? Let us see why.

Chapter 4
PER SECOND
PER SECOND

You are standing still and then begin walking down the street. At first, because you are at rest, your velocity is zero. At the end of 1 second, you are moving at a velocity of 1 foot per second. In 1 second, therefore, you have increased your velocity from zero to 1 foot per second. Your velocity keeps increasing at this steady acceleration.

At the end of the second second, your velocity is 2 feet per second. You have added another 1 foot per second to your velocity during the second second. At the end of the third second, you have added still another 1 foot per second to your velocity. Now, after 3 seconds, you are walking at a velocity of 3 feet per second.

In each second, you have increased your velocity by 1 foot per second. That is, your acceleration is 1 foot per second in each second, or 1 foot per second per second.

Accelerating car

Imagine that a car starts from rest and steadily accel-

CHANGING VELOCITY
The skier accelerates downhill. His velocity increases 5 feet per second in each second. His acceleration, therefore, is 5 feet per second per second.

ACCELERATING DOWNWARD
As the sky divers plunge towards Earth, their velocity increases. They add 32 feet per second onto their velocity in each second.

erates. After 20 seconds, it has a velocity of 40 miles/hour. What is its acceleration?

$$\text{acceleration} = \frac{\text{change in velocity}}{\text{time}}$$

$$= \frac{40 \text{ mi/hr}}{20 \text{ sec}}$$

$$= \frac{2 \text{ mi/hr}}{\text{sec}}$$

which also may be written 2 mi/hr/sec, or 2 miles per hour per second, or 2 miles per hour in each second.

At the 40 miles/hour velocity, the car increases its acceleration to 3 miles/hour/second. What is its velocity after 10 seconds? Remember that velocity = acceleration × time. The answer appears at the end of the index.

Slowing down

Acceleration can be negative. That is, an object in motion can slow down and lose velocity as well as speed up and gain velocity. When an object loses velocity, it *decelerates*.

33

Suppose that you are walking at a velocity of 3 feet per second. You begin to steadily decrease your velocity. After 1 second, your velocity is 2 feet per second. Your velocity has decreased 1 foot per second in 1 second.

You keep slowing down at the same rate. At the end of 2 seconds, your velocity has dropped to 1 foot per second. If you continue to decrease your velocity at this rate, you will stop walking in 1 more second. Your deceleration is 1 foot per second in each second, or 1 foot per second per second, or 1 ft/sec/sec.

Acceleration has direction

Let us review a few of the points we have made about velocity and acceleration. Velocity, we have said, is a vector because it has both size (speed) and direction. Any change in either speed or direction produces an acceleration. If you walk in a circular path at a constant speed, your velocity changes because your direction changes.

Since acceleration is based on velocity, it, too, is a vector. At times, therefore, accelerations are written with a direction, for example, 15 ft/sec/sec, east. The direction of an acceleration is as important as its velocity. If an acceleration occurs in the same direction in which an object moves, the velocity of the object increases. But if the acceleration occurs in the opposite direction (deceleration), the velocity of the object decreases.

Fastest man on land

Many car manufacturers emphasize the ability of certain models to accelerate quickly. A typical figure is that

SLOW DECELERATION
From the time a driver recognizes danger until he decelerates to a complete stop, a car will travel farther than many of us realize. For example:

A car moving at 30 miles/hour will take about 88 feet to stop. At double the speed, 60 miles/hour, it will stop in about 366 feet.

ROCKET SLED
Blurred motion was all that viewers could see in this dangerous acceleration experiment. The fast speedups and slowdowns of the rocket sled injured Colonel Stapp. He carried on his work to obtain information that would help space travelers, who also have to experience great accelerations.

a car standing still can accelerate to a velocity of 60 miles per hour (1 mile per minute) in 8 seconds. Let us see what the actual acceleration is.

$$\text{acceleration} = \frac{\text{change in velocity}}{\text{time}}$$

$$= \frac{60 \text{ mi/hr}}{8 \text{ sec}}$$

$$= \frac{7.5 \text{ mi/hr}}{\text{sec}}$$

Thus the car increases its velocity 7.5 miles per hour in each second. Pretty fast — but not startling in our rocket age!

In 1954, Air Force Colonel John Stapp was strapped into the seat of a rocket-driven sled mounted on a steel rail. He roared away to reach a velocity of 632 miles/hour in 5 seconds — the fastest that any man has ever traveled on the ground. What was his acceleration?

$$\text{acceleration} = \frac{\text{change in velocity}}{\text{time}}$$

$$= \frac{632 \text{ mi/hr}}{5 \text{ sec}}$$

$$= \frac{126.4 \text{ mi/hr}}{\text{sec}}$$

Although 126.4 mi/hr in each second is an almost unbelievable acceleration, the deceleration was even greater. From a velocity of 632 mi/hr, the sled stopped in only 1.1 seconds. Again, using the expression acceleration (or deceleration) = change in velocity/time, we find that deceleration = 574.5 mi/hr per second.

Galileo rejects Aristotle

We have talked mostly about the effect of acceleration on velocity. But distance depends on acceleration, too — as we shall see by going back almost 4 centuries. At that time, the famous Italian scientist Galileo Galilei was experimenting with motion at the University of Pisa.

Most of the world had grown to accept Aristotle's explanations of nature. The authority of this renowned Greek thinker (384 to 322 B.C.) spread as century after century passed — and was rarely questioned. But Galileo was an inquisitive and stubborn man. In fact, in his time he was a brilliant rebel and was regarded by many as a troublemaker. He refused to accept Aristotle's explanations of motion simply because they were traditional.

HEAVENLY MOTION
In 1609, Galileo demonstrated his first telescope. He discovered the moons of Jupiter and observed their motion. This discovery so upset the current theories of heavenly motion that many people refused to believe what they saw through the telescope. Others refused to look. But some were enthusiastic and learned.

Aristotle had written, "All men by nature desire to know." Galileo agreed but wanted to find out for himself.

The courage to experiment

Aristotle incorrectly stated that heavy objects fall faster than light objects. If he experimented with freely falling objects at all, it is not likely that he was very thorough. Greek thinkers looked down on experimentation, which they regarded as inferior to pure thought. Galileo, however, deeply believed in the value of performing experiments.

This belief required courage, for Galileo lived in an age ruled by tradition and religion. Doubters were punished, sometimes by death. But Galileo did not stop at testing Aristotle's ideas with experiments. He even challenged the practice of using the Bible to explain nature: "I think that in the discussion of natural problems we ought to begin not with the Scriptures, but with experiments, and demonstrations."

Galileo probably did not perform the famous experiment at the Leaning Tower of Pisa. The legend is that he dropped cannon balls of different weights from the top of the tower and that they struck the ground at the same time. This experiment actually may have been done by Simon Stevinus, a Dutch mathematician who lived in Galileo's time. However, Galileo did perform many experiments with falling objects. He concluded, as did Stevinus, that light and heavy objects fall at the same rate.

The inclined plane

Freely falling objects increase their velocity as they fall; that is, they accelerate. A light object with a large area — like a leaf — that is dropped does not fall freely. The air resists its motion. A leaf can only fall freely in a vacuum (a space from which the air has been removed). However, a heavy object with a small area — like a steel ball — can be considered to fall freely. The air resistance, for most experiments, is small enough to be neglected.

After Galileo had determined that objects of different weights fall freely at the same rate, he decided to investigate their acceleration. But here he had a problem. A

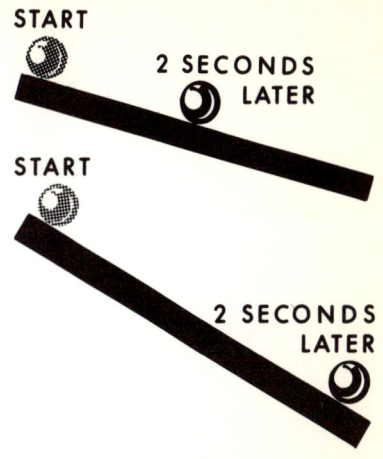

ACCELERATION VARIES WITH SLOPE
As the slope of a tilted board increases, acceleration also increases. The two balls start rolling at the same time. What happens after a given time, say 2 seconds? The ball on the steeper slope will roll farther than the other ball because its acceleration is greater.

freely falling object accelerates very rapidly, and Galileo did not have an accurate clock to measure the acceleration.

An *inclined plane* — a flat surface that is sloped (for example, a tilted board) — helped to solve the problem. The acceleration of a ball rolling down an inclined plane is considerably less than the acceleration of a ball falling freely through the air. By using an inclined plane, Galileo now had an acceleration that was slow enough to measure.

"Science came down from Heaven"

The simple board and ball contributed a new kind of knowledge — experiments that could be duplicated by others — to the study of motion. Such proof courageously rejected the mixture of tradition, religion, fact, and Greek philosophy that was the science of its day: "Science came down from Heaven to Earth on the inclined plane of Galileo."

In one series of Galileo's experiments, the interval that timed the distance the ball rolled was always the same, for example, 2 seconds. Only the acceleration was varied. As the slope of the board increased, the acceleration increased. With each increase in acceleration, the ball rolled a greater distance in the same time. What do you think Galileo observed as he decreased the slope of the board?

Galileo's formula

In another series of experiments, the slope was kept the same. Let us assume that Galileo set the slope so that

BIG DROP
Gateway Arch, in St. Louis, Missouri, is 630 feet high. Galileo's formula shows that a ball dropped from the top would travel 6.3 seconds before it hit the ground.

Such rapid accelerations were too difficult for Galileo to measure. He found it easier to experiment with inclined planes — which slowed down the motion of the balls — rather than with freely falling objects.

the ball rolled with an acceleration of 2 feet per second per second. Galileo, of course, worked with different units of measurement than we do today. But for convenience, we can select simple numbers. Why? The principle of the inclined plane is the same no matter what units of measurement are used.

At the end of each second, Galileo marked the board to show how far the ball had rolled. Here is what he found:

TIME in seconds	DISTANCE BALL ROLLED in feet
2	4
3	9
4	16

These results showed that the distance traveled by an accelerating object increases as time increases. The previous experiment had shown that the distance traveled by an accelerating object increases as acceleration increases. Galileo combined the results of both experiments in a single conclusion: Distance equals one-half the acceleration multiplied by time multiplied by time again, which can be written

distance = ½ acceleration × time × time

Test Galileo's formula, using the figures in the chart. Remember that acceleration equals 2 feet per second per second.

Dropping through the air

Galileo's formula applies to a freely falling object as well as to a ball rolling down an inclined plane. Say that we want to find the depth of a well. We can drop a stone into the well, and while it is falling we can count seconds until we hear the splash. Then we can apply Galileo's formula to find the distance to the water.

DIVIDE BY 2

You can find how high a ball is thrown with Galileo's formula. When you time the flight, remember: The time it takes the ball to reach its greatest height equals the time it takes to come down. Therefore, divide the total time the ball spends in the air by 2.

We require 2 facts: time and acceleration. Let us assume that we hear the splash of the stone 2 seconds after it is dropped. Experiments show that a freely falling object accelerates at 32 feet per second per second. As we previously noted, air resists the motion of objects that move through it. However, a heavy object with a small area, like a stone, is not slowed very much by the air. We can, therefore, ignore air resistance in this example and apply Galileo's formula. We can also ignore the short time it takes for the sound of the splash to travel up the well. Note: Distance is in feet, acceleration in feet per second per second, and time in seconds.

$$\begin{aligned} \text{distance} &= \tfrac{1}{2} \text{ acceleration} \times \text{time} \times \text{time} \\ &= \tfrac{1}{2}\, 32 \times 2 \times 2 \\ &= 16 \times 4 \\ &= 64 \end{aligned}$$

The distance from the top of the well to the water, therefore, is 64 feet. What is the distance if the splash is heard after 1 second? After 3 seconds? Work with Galileo's formula, and check your answers against those given at the end of the index.

Chapter 5
FORCE — THE MOVER

Have you ever been to the Olympic Games or watched them on television? Athletes spring over hurdles, pole vault through the air, knife through the water, hurl javelins, flex muscles, exert forces, throw balls, lift weights, dash, and run — to mention just some of the sights that are to be seen. Everywhere you look, athletes and objects are in motion, and forces are constantly being exerted.

Start, stop, or alter

What is force? When we exert a force on an object, we push or pull it, bend, break, twist, or squeeze it. But

FORCES IN ACTION
Three different effects of force are demonstrated in these pictures. The ball is distorted — that is, its shape is changed — by the tennis racket. The light bulb is smashed by the hammer blow. The diver flips through the air because he pushed down, causing the board to push up.

EXPERIMENTAL TRIP
We are going to use a bicycle like this in an interesting thought experiment that will show how force affects motion. First a single rider will pedal, then 2, and then 3.

what is more important in the study of motion, we may move the object. Gravitational force pulls all objects towards the center of the Earth. And magnetic forces reach out across space to pull iron objects towards the magnet.

Force is any push or pull that tends to start, stop, or alter the motion of an object. We have said that any change in motion is acceleration. Thus a force applied to an object tends to accelerate it.

Like velocity and acceleration, force is a vector. Its complete description requires direction as well as size. When a force acts in the direction of motion, it produces acceleration. When a force acts opposite to the direction of motion, it produces deceleration. When a force acts across the direction of motion, it changes that direction. This change causes acceleration or deceleration.

Distance increases as acceleration increases

Suppose we try an experiment to see how force produces acceleration. Imagine that 3 riders make several trips down a straight road on a bicycle-built-for-3. The 3 riders are the same weight, and each can apply the same

42

force to the pedals. All trips will begin from rest with all 3 riders aboard.

Galileo found that in a given time interval, distance increases as acceleration increases. He further learned that when acceleration doubles, distance doubles; when acceleration triples, distance triples; and so on. If we compare the distances covered in each trip, we can then compare the accelerations. The time interval for each trip will be constant: 1 minute.

Distance increases as force increases

On the first trip, only 1 rider pedals. On the second trip, 2 riders pedal, and all 3 riders pedal on the third trip. This arrangement provides for a continuous increase in force: Force doubles on the second trip and triples on the third trip. Let us see how distance and acceleration change.

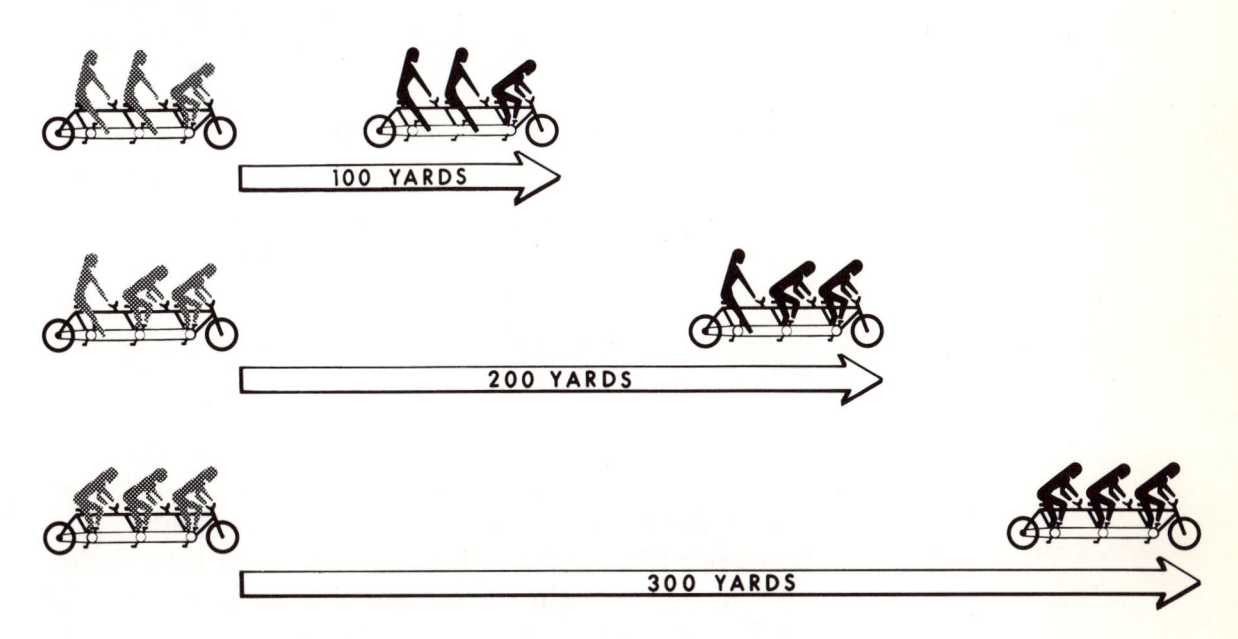

If your guess is that distance increases as force does, you are right. The distance covered on the second trip — when force doubles — is 2 times the distance covered on the first trip. Similarly, the distance covered on the third trip — when force triples — is 3 times that of the first trip. Remember that all 3 riders are on the bicycle for each trip. Therefore, the weight of the bicycle stays the same throughout this experiment.

43

BURST OF DISCOVERY

Isaac Newton wrote most of his great works on motion in the short period of 2 years — during a time that he spent in the country to escape the plague in London. When he started this study, Newton was 23 years old.

How force influences motion

What happens to the acceleration of the bicycle when more riders pedal, that is, when force increases? For the answer, let us turn to Isaac Newton (1642-1727), the great English physicist who performed numerous experiments to learn how force influences motion. Newton, who was born in the year of Galileo's death, continued Galileo's great work on motion.

As a result of his experiments, Newton observed: "If any force generates a motion, a double force will generate double the motion, a triple force triple the motion. . . ." If we substitute *acceleration* for *motion,* we have the answer to our question — acceleration increases directly as the force that produces it increases.

Mass never varies

We know that it is harder to push a heavy object than it is to push a light one. Thus heaviness as well as force affects motion. Can we use weight as a measure of heaviness when we discuss acceleration?

44

The answer is no, because weight varies from place to place. An object will have a different weight at sea level, on a mountain top, and in a high-flying airplane. We shall find out why in this chapter. Since weight is variable, we require a measurement of heaviness that is constant. We have one — it is called *mass*.

Have you ever placed a football on the ground, gotten a good running start, then kicked the ball and watched it soar? It is not likely that you would ever attempt to kick a bowling ball the same way. The bowling ball is denser than the football; that is, it has more matter. *Mass is a measure of the quantity of matter in a body.* We pointed out that weight varies with distance from sea level. However, since the quantity of matter in a body is always the same, mass never varies.

Only 1 rider pedals

In the last bicycle experiment, 3 riders went on every trip. First, 1 rider pedaled, then 2, and then 3. Thus acceleration was changed by keeping mass constant and

DENSITY

Each of these blocks has the same length, width, and height — and, therefore, the same volume. But they do not contain the same amount of matter.

The lead block has the greatest amount of matter, that is, mass. The aluminum block has the least, and the iron block is in between.

Which material has the greatest density? Lead — because it has more matter than the other 2 blocks, which are of equal volume.

varying force. Now let us see what happens to acceleration when we reverse these conditions: Force will be constant and mass will vary. Each trip will take the same amount of time, and only 1 rider will pedal to keep force constant.

We are on the way. Remember that all 3 riders have the same mass. The first trip has 1 rider; the second has 2 riders; and the third has 3 riders. Therefore, mass doubles on the second trip and triples on the third trip.

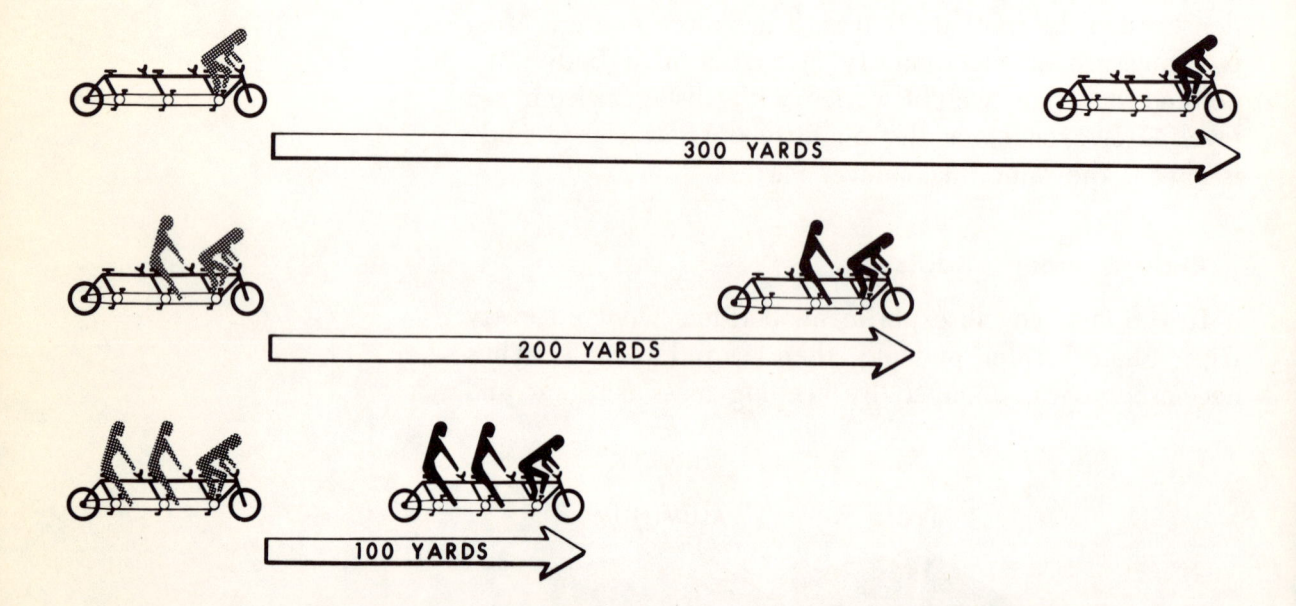

300 YARDS

200 YARDS

100 YARDS

How do the distances compare? The distance covered on the first trip is double that covered on the second trip. It is triple that covered on the third trip.

How do the accelerations compare? Keep in mind that distance increases or decreases as acceleration increases or decreases. By comparing distances, therefore, we can compare accelerations. This comparison answers our question: If a single force is acting (1 rider pedaling), acceleration decreases when mass increases.

The Second Law

Isaac Newton carried out experiments similar in principle to our bicycle experiment. Working with different forces acting on different masses, he concluded: The acceleration of a moving body increases when the force acting on the body increases. Further, when a single force acts on a moving body, acceleration decreases as the mass of the body increases. These statements, together, are known as Newton's Second Law of Motion. (We will look into the first and third laws later.)

Laws in society are man-made. But laws in science are discovered. They describe what always takes place in nature under certain conditions.

We can express the second law as acceleration equals force divided by mass, or

$$\text{acceleration} = \frac{\text{force}}{\text{mass}}$$

We can also say that force equals mass times acceleration, or

$$\text{force} = \text{mass} \times \text{acceleration}$$

How to compare measurements

Up to this point, we have included units with measurements. We have expressed measurements of time, for example, in seconds or minutes; measurements of length in feet or miles. In solving problems, we have come up with answers like this: The velocity of the first car is 50 miles/hour, and the velocity of the second car is 25 miles/hour. However, units are not necessary if we only want to *compare* the velocities of the 2 cars. In this instance, we can say: The velocity of the first car is 50/25, or 2, times faster than the velocity of the second car.

This approach is helpful when any of the units are complicated. In the Second Law of Motion, we are dealing with force, mass, and acceleration. We could use pounds to measure force. Acceleration, as we know, is often measured in feet per second per second. But mass presents a problem — its units are not simple to work with.

We can bypass this problem, however, since we want to compare measurements under different conditions. For example, let us see what happens to acceleration in the Second Law of Motion when we keep force constant and increase mass.

MEASUREMENT
This bird can be scientifically described with units of measurement. For example:
▶ Size in inches.
▶ Weight in ounces.
▶ Velocity in feet/second.
▶ Body temperature in degrees.
▶ Age in years.

force	=	mass	×	acceleration
12	=	1	×	12
12	=	2	×	6
12	=	6	×	2
12	=	12	×	1

MASS VS. ACCELERATION
A good college athlete can put (throw) a 16-pound shot about 50 feet. He can put a 12-pound shot about 62 feet. The lighter (less massive) shot has less resistance to change in motion. It can be given a greater acceleration and will travel farther.

The chart shows that as mass increases, acceleration decreases.

Now let us switch and keep mass constant and increase force.

force	=	mass	×	acceleration
6	=	3	×	2
12	=	3	×	4
18	=	3	×	6
24	=	3	×	8

This time, the chart shows that as force increases, acceleration increases. In fact, as we have observed before, if force doubles, acceleration doubles; and if force triples, acceleration triples.

Mass resists change of motion

In the second bicycle experiment, only the first rider pedaled — first himself, then with 1 more rider, and finally with 2 more riders. It became more difficult for the first rider to accelerate the bicycle each time a new rider got on — that is, when the mass increased. You may have had a similar experience if you have ever carried a passenger or a heavy package on a bicycle.

With each new rider, it also became more difficult to

(continued on page 61)

a picture gallery of motion

what is an axis?

It is an imaginary line around which a body turns. An "axle," however, is an actual rod or shaft around which a body turns. The imaginary line of an axis runs through the length of an axle. Thus an axle is, in a sense, a real axis. Car, carriage, and bicycle wheels rotate on axles.

The metal cylinder was spun around an axle at enormous speed. The resulting centrifugal force pushed out from the center of the cylinder. This force was greater than the strength of the cylinder and caused it to split apart.

The same body can turn around different axes. Pencil A turns on an axis (dotted line) through its length. If it were lying on a table, it would roll. Pencil B turns on an axis like a propeller. Pencil C turns on an axis through its end, moving like a clock hand.

The Earth has an axis (dotted line) that passes through its center. As you can see, the axis is tilted and runs between north and south. The Earth spins like a top. Every object on it takes a complete circular trip once every 24 hours.

The largest circular path is at the Equator. A man living there travels farther in 24 hours than a man living any other place — as shown in the drawing.

Which man is traveling faster? The answer is the man at the Equator. Both men travel for the same length of time, but the man at the Equator travels a greater distance. The only way he can do this is to travel faster than the other man. We can therefore conclude that circular speed at the Equator is greater than elsewhere on Earth.

51

adventure in motion

Who can look the other way when a man is in motion? He is bound to capture our interest whether he is a runner, a 16th century explorer, an astronaut, a legend, or a character in a book. Phileas Fogg was such a man. He journeyed into the public's imagination in 1873 as the fictional hero of Jules Verne's book "Around the World in 80 Days."

At that time, circling the world in 80 days would have been considered a great accomplishment. Although nobody was sure that such fast travel was possible, Verne was proved to be correct. Shortly after the book was published, a New York newspaperwoman, Nellie Bly, made the trip in 77 days.

Like all adventurers on the move, Phileas Fogg traveled on any transportation he could find. Some of the vehicles he used and their approximate speeds are shown on these pages. A jet plane, in a record flight, made the same trip in less than 2 days. Both trips were governed by the laws of motion and the urgings of the human spirit.

Balloon — about 20 miles/hour

Train — about 50 miles/hour

Elephant — about 6 miles/hour

Ship — about 10 miles/hour

Wind Wagon — about 7 miles/hour

Ostrich Cart — about 8 miles/hour

53

subatomic motion

Scientists who are interested in the atom often split its nucleus — the heavy core that contains most of the mass. They split the nucleus by bombarding it with atomic projectiles, such as protons (the nuclei of hydrogen atoms).

The atomic projectiles are accelerated to enormous speeds — near that of light — in machines called particle accelerators. After the particles reach the correct speed and momentum, they are guided to strike their targets — the substance being studied.

Some target atoms are split apart by the collision. As a result, subatomic particles (smaller than an atom) fly out from the nuclei of the split atoms.

Subatomic particles are too small and travel too fast to be seen by eye. But their motion can be made to produce a visible vapor trail, like that of a jet plane. For this purpose, they are next passed through a large tank called a bubble chamber. The chamber contains hydrogen — ordinarily a gas — cooled to a liquid state.

As the particles speed through the chamber, they produce tiny bubbles of vapor in the liquid hydrogen. Each type of particle creates a vapor trail with its own distinct shape. Photographs taken through a window in the chamber help scientists identify the particles that make the trails.

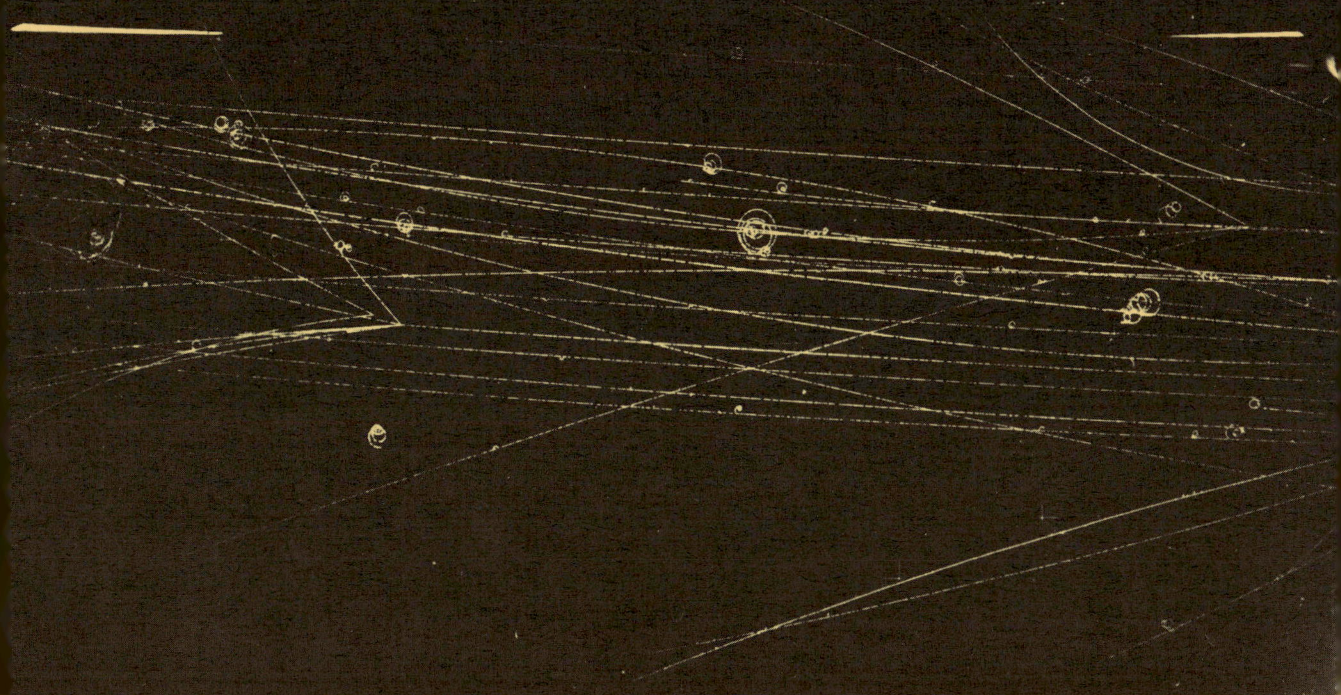

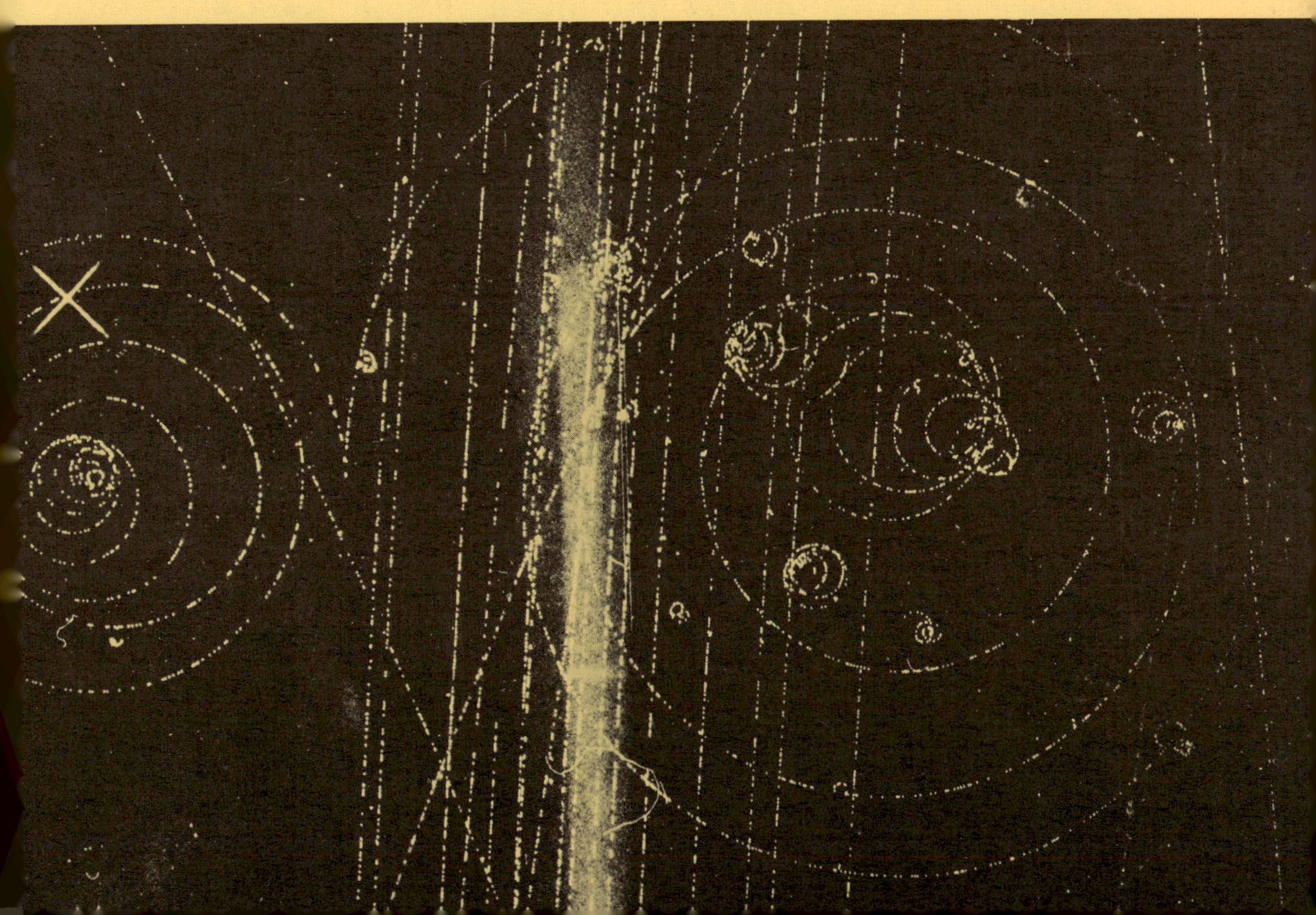

City traffic jam

Tokyo-Osaka Express

Seattle monorail

ground transportation

More and more people and goods are being transported in and out of cities. This growing traffic — and the jams it causes — is now a major problem in the United States and elsewhere. The roads, harbors, railroads, and airports that we use today were designed for yesterday's transportation needs.

Some new approaches to transportation, however, are being developed. One of the most successful of these is the high-speed train. The Tokyo-Osaka Express, for example, carries passengers between these 2 cities at speeds over 100 miles/hour. Such trains have been proposed to link major cities in the United States.

The monorail in Seattle, Washington, is a train running on a single rail that is raised above the streets. It speeds passengers at 50 miles/hour across the city in minutes. Monorails may one day reduce traffic snarls by connecting cities with suburbs and airports.

Engineers are experimenting with tubeflight trains for future travel. These trains will be propelled through giant tubes by jets of air ejected from the back. The tubes protect the trains from bad weather and can be located above or below the ground. Tubeflight trains will be noiseless and will travel as fast as 375 miles/hour. At this speed a trip from Washington, D.C., to New York City would take about 35 minutes.

Another use of air for transportation is over water. The Hydroskimmer, for example, is an air cushion vehicle that can travel over 80 miles/hour. It floats above the water on a cushion of air that is created by 4 fans set into the hull. Forward motion is provided by 2 propellers mounted on the rear. The Hydroskimmer in the photograph is 65 feet long by 27 feet wide. Larger air cushion vehicles are planned for ocean travel.

Proposed design for tubeflight train

Hydroskimmer air cushion vehicle

flights of imagination

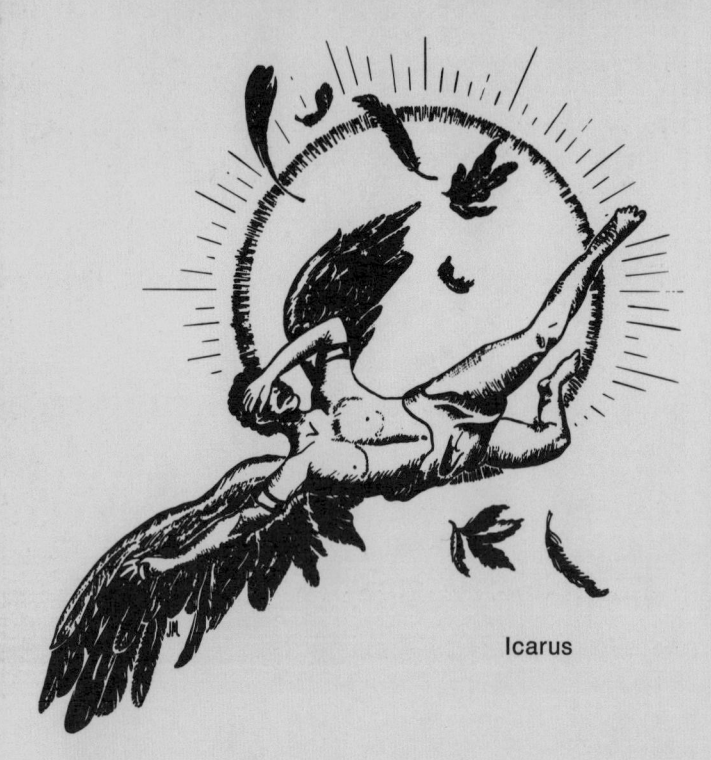

A Greek legend several thousand years old tells of the miraculous escape from a prison tower by Daedalus and his son, Icarus. They flew from the tower with artificial wings made of wax and feathers. Not heeding his father's warning, Icarus flew too near the Sun. His wings melted, and he fell into the sea.

In the 15th century, this idea was reborn in the mind of Leonardo da Vinci. He believed that man could fly by copying the motion of birds: "A bird is an instrument working according to mathematical law, which . . . is within the capacity of man to reproduce."

Unfortunately, his design for a flying machine was impractical. Humans do not have the strength to operate such huge

Icarus

Flying machine

wings. But his helicopter — the design was based on a toy from the Orient — would have flown if a powerful enough engine had existed to drive it.

Man's desire to conquer the air continued after Leonardo. In 1843, posters of a large flying steam locomotive shown soaring over the Egyptian pyramids appeared in London. The posters were an advertisement of the Aerial Transit Company, which had designed and built this modern looking, propeller-driven craft.

Because its engine was too heavy, the flying steam locomotive never got off the ground. It was, however, another step towards realizing man's ancient dream: powered flight, finally achieved by the Wright brothers in 1903.

Helicopter

Flying steam locomotive

motion of a splash

seen by a camera, predicted by a computer

Here in the land of splashes, a high-speed camera photographed a crown decorated with pearls. It was produced by a milk drop splashing into a thin layer of milk. The drawing created by the computer is remarkably similar.

Scientists are working with computers to predict and draw many other motion situations. For example:

▶ Automobile crashes, to design safer cars.

▶ Rocket flights, to plot the paths of space voyages.

▶ Air currents and cloud movements, to understand and forecast the weather.

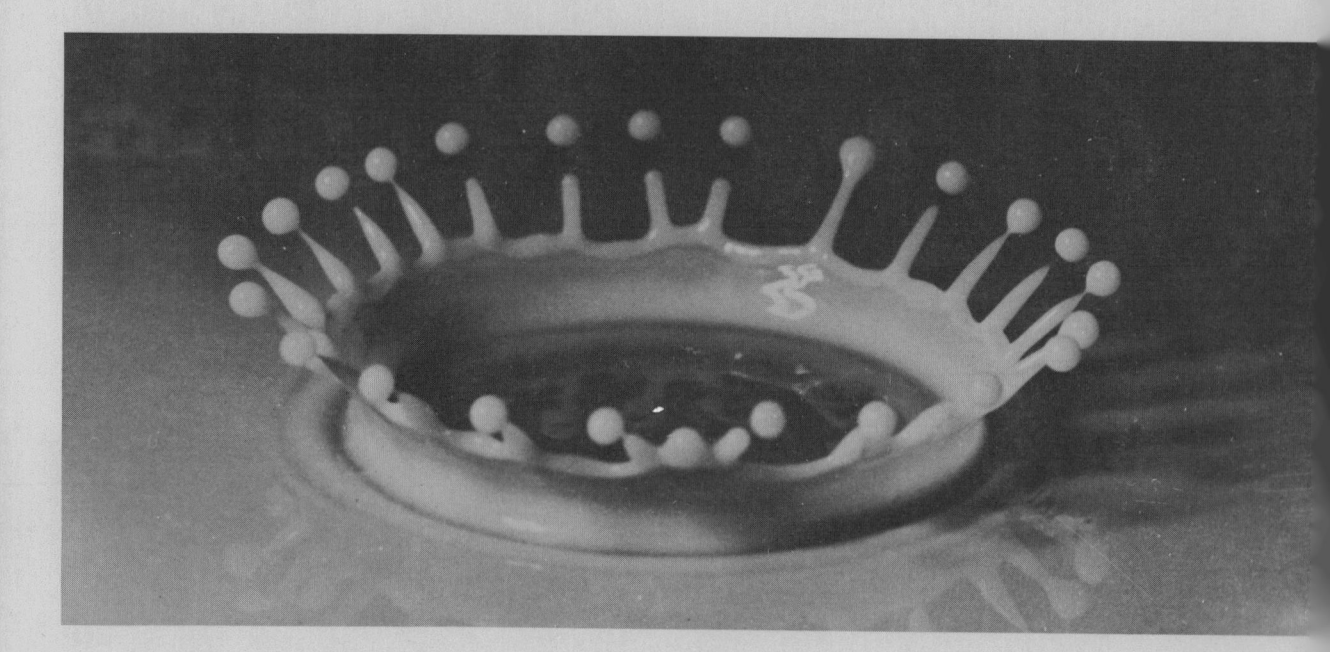

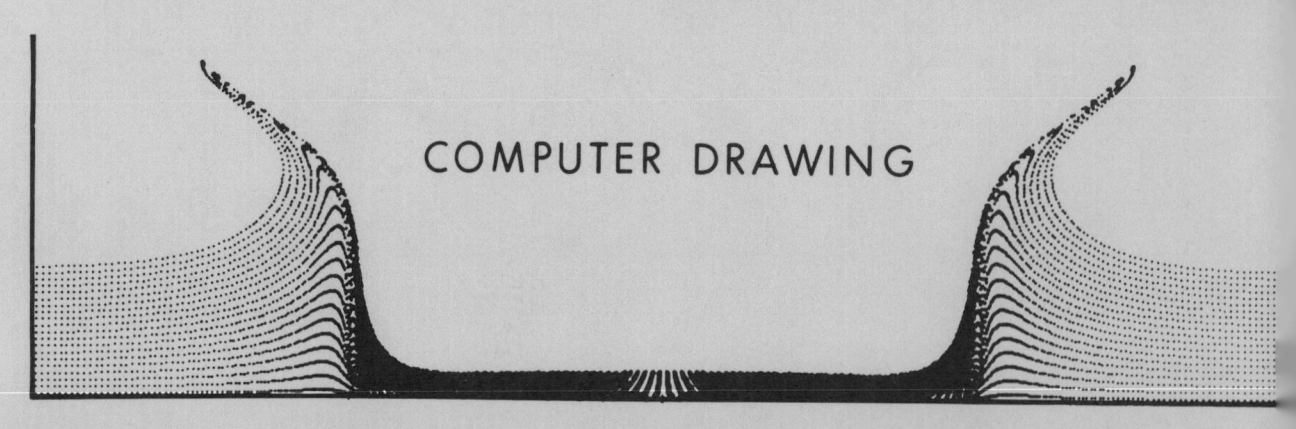

COMPUTER DRAWING

(continued from page 48)

start the bicycle moving. A similar situation exists if a sports car and a large truck are standing at a traffic light that has just turned green. The sports car darts ahead while the truck is just beginning to roll slowly. Or consider a football and a bowling ball. If you kick the football, it will accelerate rapidly into the air. But if you kick the bowling ball, it will resist your foot and, at best, accelerate just a few feet along the ground.

Mass always resists a change in motion. The mass may be at rest (zero velocity) and resist moving. Or it may be moving and resist increasing or decreasing its velocity. Since any change in velocity is an acceleration, we can also say that mass resists acceleration.

Hard to start, hard to stop

Large masses have greater resistance to a change in motion than small masses. It is harder to start a truck moving from rest than it is a sports car. If they are both moving at the same speed, it is harder to slow down the truck than it is to slow down the sports car by an equal amount. The reverse is also true. It is harder to speed up the truck than it is to speed up the sports car by an equal amount.

A change in motion may mean a change in direction.

DIFFERENT INERTIAS
Almost immediately after blastoff, the small rocket is on its way up through the atmosphere. The large rocket has enormous inertia. It lifts only a short distance from the launching pad in the same time. When you next see a large rocket launched on television, observe how slowly it lifts at first.

A moving mass, therefore, also resists any change in the direction of its motion. The sports car can whip around a sharp curve. If the truck attempts to take the same curve at the same speed, it may skid or turn over. The large mass of the truck tends to carry it straight ahead in the direction of its motion.

Inertia

The property that matter has that causes it to resist a change in motion is called *inertia*. By this, we mean that a body at rest tends to stay at rest. And a body at constant velocity tends to keep moving at constant velocity. We will explore these ideas further at the beginning of the next chapter.

Right now let us pursue the relationship between inertia and mass. We have considered mass to be a measure of the amount of matter in a body. Mass is also a measure of the amount of the inertia of a body — that is, it measures how strongly a body resists changing its state of motion.

FORCE WITHOUT MOTION The force of the karate blow splits the watermelon instead of moving it. The melon's large mass resists any change in motion. This blow would move a football instead of splitting it. Why?

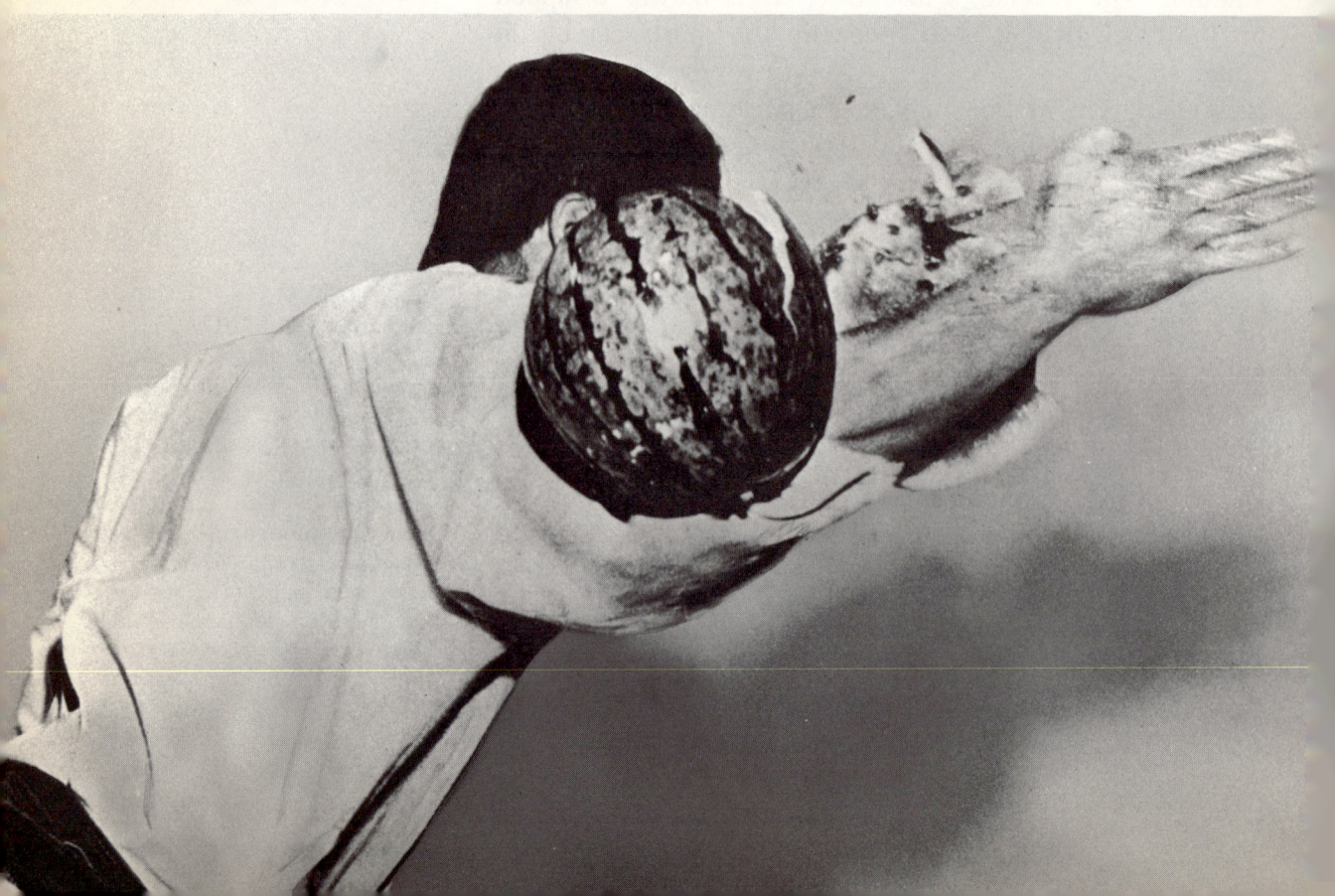

In order to change a body's motion, force is needed to overcome the body's inertia. Any change in motion, however — speeding up, slowing down, or taking a new direction — produces an acceleration. We can conclude, therefore, that mass measures the amount of force necessary to produce an acceleration.

Value of a broad approach

We have described mass in 3 different ways:

▶ A measure of the amount of matter in a body.
▶ A measure of the amount of inertia in a body.
▶ A measure of the amount of force necessary to produce an acceleration in a body.

All 3 descriptions of mass are useful. This approach — working with more than one description — is often helpful in science. Sometimes a particular description is more suitable for one problem than another. That is, it may make that problem easier to understand. For example, if we are concerned with motion, we may want to consider how mass influences acceleration. Or if we are involved in a gravity problem, we may find it helpful to regard mass as the amount of matter in a body.

Towards the center of the Earth

Gravity, one of the great forces in nature, continuously acts on every living and nonliving thing. It has been called "the glue that binds the universe together, keeping everything — from pebbles to planets — in its place." Most of the time we are interested in the effects of gravity on our planet and on the space surrounding it. We will therefore consider *gravity* to be the force of attraction between any mass and Earth.

When we *weigh* a mass, we measure this force, which pulls the mass towards the center of the Earth. Earlier we said that mass is better than weight as a measure of a body's heaviness. The reason this is so, as Isaac Newton observed, is that the attractive force of gravity weakens as distances increase. The distance is measured on a

DOWNWARD PULL
How many examples can you think of that show matter being pulled towards the center of the Earth?

straight line from the center of the body to the center of the Earth.

The Earth, however, has an irregular surface. Consider 2 men, 1 standing on top of Mt. Everest and the other on an ocean beach. Which man is pulled by a greater gravitational force? The answer appears at the end of the index.

Moreover, the Earth is like a ball that is flattened at the poles and bulges at the Equator. The distance from the North and South Poles to the Earth's center is less than the distance from the Equator to the Earth's center. Imagine that you weighed yourself at the Equator and then took a jet to the North Pole and weighed yourself there. You would weigh slightly more at the North Pole than at the Equator because the North Pole is closer to the center of the Earth than is the Equator.

Now we can see why mass is better than weight as a measure of a body's heaviness. Your mass, or the amount of matter in your body, was the same at both the North Pole and the Equator. But your weight was different at each place — and this difference makes weight a less reliable measurement than mass.

Why Galileo was right

You may be wondering why (as Galileo showed) large and small masses fall at the same acceleration. Let us look into the reason. We know that a mass accelerates when a force acts on it. If the mass doubles, the force must double to produce the same acceleration. Since the masses are falling, the force acting on them is gravity.

Imagine that you and your father are skydiving — jumping out of an airplane and falling freely for a few moments before opening your parachutes. You both jump together. We will examine what happens only during the period of free fall.

Your mass is such that the Earth pulls on you with a force of 100 pounds. This force (gravity) causes you to accelerate at 32 feet per second per second. Your father has twice your mass, so that gravity pulls on him with a force of 200 pounds.

His inertia is also twice as large as yours. Remember that inertia is the property of matter that causes it to resist a change in motion. Gravity, acting on your father, has to overcome twice the inertia that you have. While he falls, twice the force is being applied to twice the mass. Both of you therefore have the same amount of force applied to each particle of mass in your bodies. The result is that you each fall at the same acceleration: 32 feet per second per second.

DROPPED AT THE SAME TIME
According to Aristotle, which will reach the ground first, the vase or the statue?

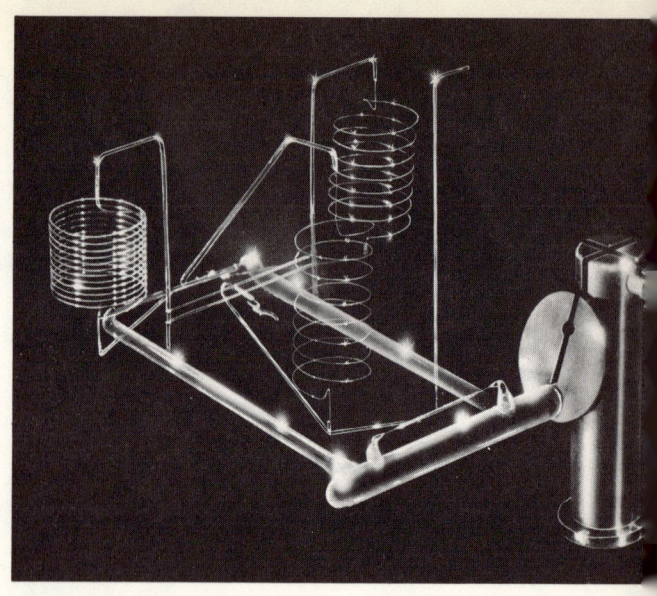

MEASURING GRAVITY

The gravity meters, used by these army technicians, can detect minute changes in the pull of gravity at different locations.

Inside each meter, a system of 3 delicate springs acts like an extremely sensitive weighing scale. The pointer of the scale is the thin vertical rod, on the right, with the bend at the top.

Pushing with twice the force

After the skydive, the next suggested trip is on the ground. This ride offers another way to understand why different masses fall at the same acceleration. Picture yourself in a cart on smooth pavement. (The cart is made of a strong, light plastic. We can ignore its mass, which is small compared to yours.) A friend is pushing the cart at a certain acceleration. After he stops the cart, you leave and your father takes your place. As in the skydiving example, your father has twice your mass.

Off they go. Your friend pushes harder and harder, and the cart accelerates faster and faster. Finally, your friend is pushing with twice the force he exerted when you were in the cart. His force overcomes twice your inertia. The cart's acceleration, however, is the same as when you were inside. This situation closely resembles the skydive. Then, while you and your father were falling freely, you both also had the same acceleration.

Upside down numbers

Now and then, we have turned to mathematics to help us look more deeply into motion. We shall, at this point, investigate a new mathematical idea — the inverse. This idea will be valuable in understanding more about motion, especially the simple beauty of one of Isaac Newton's discoveries.

An *inverse* is a number that is turned upside down. The inverse of a whole number, like 5, is 1/5. Where does the 1 come from? Actually, 5 can be regarded as 5 divided by 1 or 5/1, because any number divided by 1 is equal to itself.

The inverse of 3, therefore, is 1/3; of 2 is 1/2; and of 50 is 1/50. Fractions are handled the same way — they are turned upside down. The inverse of 3/4 is 4/3; of 2/3 is 3/2; and of 1/2 is 2/1, or 2. The inverse of a number is also called its *reciprocal*. Both terms are widely used in science and have the same meaning.

Far from the surface

We have discussed Newton's observation that gravitational attraction decreases with increasing distance from the center of the Earth. The attraction can be measured by weight or acceleration. It is inversely related to the distance multiplied by itself. This inverse expression is written

$$\frac{1}{\text{distance} \times \text{distance}}$$

The distance from the surface of the Earth to its center — although it varies from place to place — is approximately 4,000 miles. Assume that an astronaut is 4,000 miles in space. His distance from the center of the Earth has, therefore, doubled. His weight and acceleration are $\frac{1}{2 \times 2}$, or $\frac{1}{4}$, of their values at sea level. If he triples his distance, his weight and acceleration are $\frac{1}{3 \times 3}$, or $\frac{1}{9}$, of their values at sea level.

What are the weight and acceleration of a 160-pound astronaut who has doubled his distance from the center of the Earth?

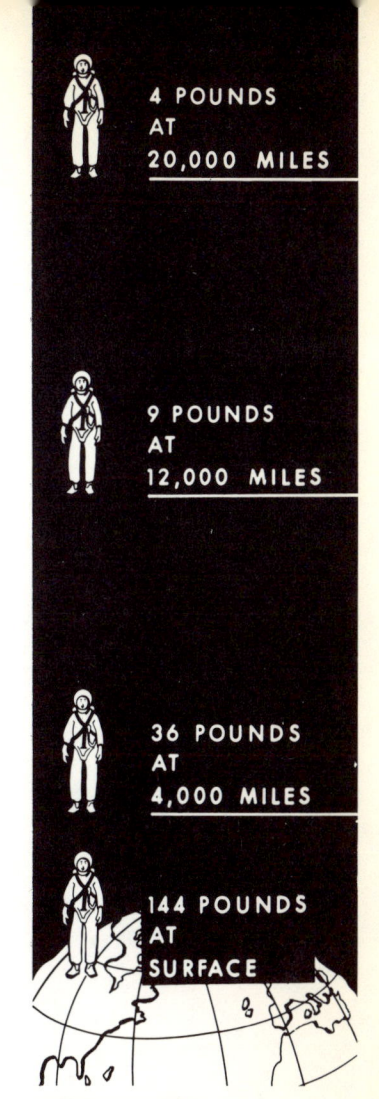

4 POUNDS AT 20,000 MILES

9 POUNDS AT 12,000 MILES

36 POUNDS AT 4,000 MILES

144 POUNDS AT SURFACE

WEIGHT LOSS
The man's mass never changes. His weight, however, decreases as his distance from the Earth's center increases. Apply the formula discussed in the text, and see if you can obtain the same weights as those shown in the drawing.

The distances shown in the drawing are from the surface of the Earth. Remember that the formula calls for distance from the center of the Earth. Thus 12,000 miles above the surface equals 16,000 miles above the center — or 4 times the distance from the center to the surface.

$$\text{weight} = \frac{1}{2 \times 2} \times 160 \text{ pounds}$$

$$= 40 \text{ pounds}$$

$$\text{acceleration} = \frac{1}{2 \times 2} \times 32 \text{ feet per second per second}$$

$$= 8 \text{ feet per second per second}$$

What is the weight of a 160-pound astronaut who is 16,000 miles from the surface of the Earth? The answer appears at the end of the index.

WEIGHT ON OTHER PLANETS

Suppose an astronaut who weighs 150 pounds on Earth could travel to the other planets. His weight would change wherever he went, as shown in the drawing.

The drawing also shows the sizes (not the masses) of the different planets compared to one another. The mass of each planet determines its gravitational force — and the weight of the astronaut.

MERCURY	54 POUNDS
VENUS	129 POUNDS
EARTH	150 POUNDS
MOON	25 POUNDS
MARS	60 POUNDS
JUPITER	396 POUNDS
SATURN	180 POUNDS
URANUS	138 POUNDS
NEPTUNE	168 POUNDS
PLUTO	NOT KNOWN

Tug of war

We defined gravity as the force of attraction between any mass and the Earth. The word *between* is important because it means that gravity is not a one-way pull. It is more like a tug of war. The Earth, for example, pulls on you, and you pull on the Earth — and both pulls (forces) are equal.

The Earth pulls on a large mass with a greater force than it pulls on a small mass. This is why large masses weigh more than small masses. If you stand on a scale, the dial shows a certain weight that is a result of the gravitational force between you and the Earth. If a heavier friend stands on the scale, the gravitational force between him and the Earth is larger. He is pulled towards the center of the Earth with a force greater than the force that pulled you. The result is that he presses on the platform of the scale harder than you did — and the dial reads a higher weight.

Like the Earth, the Moon exerts a gravitational force. However, the mass of the Moon is much smaller than that of the Earth. The pull of gravity on the Moon is 6 times weaker than the pull of gravity on the Earth. A woman weighing 120 pounds on Earth would weigh 120/6, or 20, pounds on the moon.

Every body attracts every other body

Newton's work led him to conclude that gravitational attraction is universal — that is, it exists everywhere, including the Earth, Sun, Moon, planets, stars, and all other bodies throughout the heavens. Thus every body in the universe attracts every other body in the universe. While you are reading, you are exerting a gravitational force on the book, on other objects and people in the room, and on the most distant heavenly bodies in the universe. And all of these are exerting a gravitational force on you.

Much of Newton's brilliant work on motion was summarized in his Universal Law of Gravitation, which states:

▶ All bodies in the universe attract each other.

▶ The force of attraction between 2 bodies increases as the mass of either or both increases.

▶ The force of attraction between 2 bodies decreases as the distance between them increases. This force is inversely related to the distance multiplied by itself.

The Universal Law is one of the great discoveries of science. For this and his other insights into nature, Newton is regarded by some as the finest scientific thinker who ever lived. The poet Alexander Pope said of him:

*Nature and Nature's laws lay hid in night:
God said, Let Newton be! and all was light.*

Newton, however, was all too aware that nature had countless puzzles that were still to be solved. Towards the end of his life, he summed up his work in simple language that is still moving: "I do not know what I may appear to the world; but to myself I seem to have been only like a boy playing on the seashore, and diverting myself in now and then finding a smoother pebble or a prettier shell than ordinary, while the great ocean of truth lay all undiscovered before me."

MUTUAL ATTRACTION
A comet pulls on other heavenly bodies — like the Sun and planets — and they pull on it. These forces of attraction influence the path the comet follows as it blazes through the heavens.

Chapter 6
ENDLESS MOTION?

The bus you are standing in stops, and you tend to fall forward. When the bus starts again, you tend to fall backward. Each time the bus stops or starts, you tend to resist the change in motion. What can we conclude?

Recall that inertia is the tendency of a body (in this case, you) to resist any change in motion. With this in mind, your experience on the bus leads us to conclude: Because of inertia, a body that is moving tends to keep moving. Similarly, because of inertia, a body that is at rest tends to remain at rest.

Galileo would have agreed with this conclusion because it verifies what he learned in experiments with balls rolling down inclined planes. So far so good — but let us go 1 step farther. Let us see how Galileo might analyze another present-day experience that is related to his work: It is a bright winter day, and the ground is covered with snow. Three friends, Wes, Rhonda, and Edith are standing on a hill with their sleds — and off they go.

SAFETY IDEAS FROM A SMASH UP
The test car is about to crash. The dummies in the car are built to react like a human body. The results of the tests — which investigate motion features like inertia and acceleration — guide engineers in designing safer cars.

Inertia on a hill

Wes glided down the hill onto a level stretch of ground. Then he rode up a second hill that was just as steep as the first one. He coasted to a stop at the same height he started from on the first hill.

Rhonda went downhill in a different direction. After riding on level ground, she came to a hill that was less steep than the first. Up she went, coasting a longer distance than Wes did. But she, too, stopped at the same height she started from.

Edith, who rode down the hill in a third direction, did not find another hill to go up. Instead, she kept coasting on level ground. When did she stop? How far uphill did Wes and Rhonda travel? Suppose we let Galileo tell us.

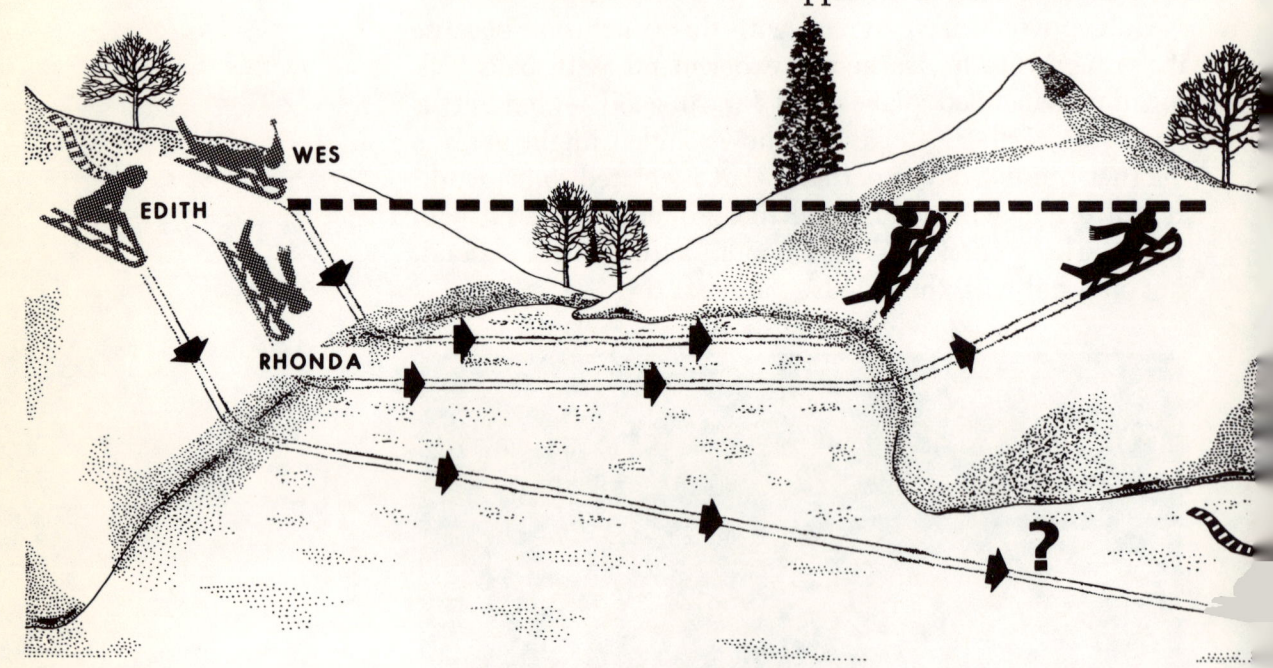

Gravity pulls straight down

If Galileo were watching, he would point out that all 3 sleds were accelerated by gravity on the way down. The rate of acceleration was the same for each because they all went down the same hill. He would remind us that gravity pulls straight down. The hill prevented the sleds from traveling straight down, so that Wes, Rhonda, and Edith did not accelerate as rapidly as would a freely falling body.

Galileo would perhaps then observe that when the sleds

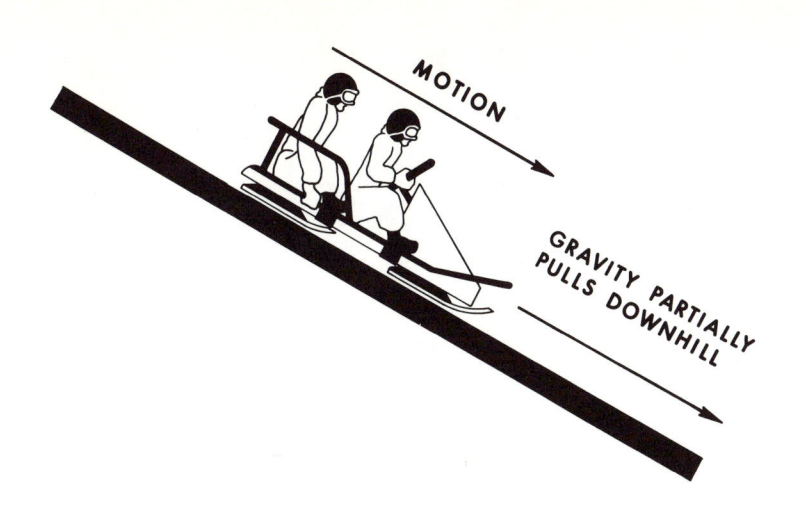

ACCELERATION
Bobsled traveling downhill: The force of gravity partially pulls in the same direction as the motion of the sled — downhill. The sled, therefore, accelerates (increases its velocity).

rode on level ground, gravity did not affect their forward motion. Again, the reason is that gravity only pulls in a downward direction. But when Wes and Rhonda rode uphill, the sleds decelerated. Why? "È ovvio!" Galileo would probably reply. "La gravita si oppone al suo moto." A translation appears at the end of the index.

For the present, we are ignoring the effect of friction. This force, created when 2 surfaces rub against each other, would oppose the motion of the sleds and slow them down. However, like Galileo and his inclined plane, we want to consider only the effect of the force of gravity on motion.

To equal heights

As Wes came down the hill, his sled accelerated because of the pull of gravity. On the level ground, his sled moved at constant velocity because it was not opposed or helped by any force. (Remember that we are ignoring friction. And gravity only acts straight down — not in a horizontal, or level, direction.)

When Wes started to go up another hill, the force of gravity once again was felt. Since both hills had the same steepness, he decelerated at the same rate going up as he had coming down. He therefore traveled to a height on the second hill that was equal to the height he had started from on the first hill.

CONSTANT VELOCITY
Bobsled traveling on level ground: No forces act either in the direction of motion or in the opposite direction. The sled, therefore, travels at constant velocity (does not accelerate or decelerate). Friction is neglected in this and similar examples.

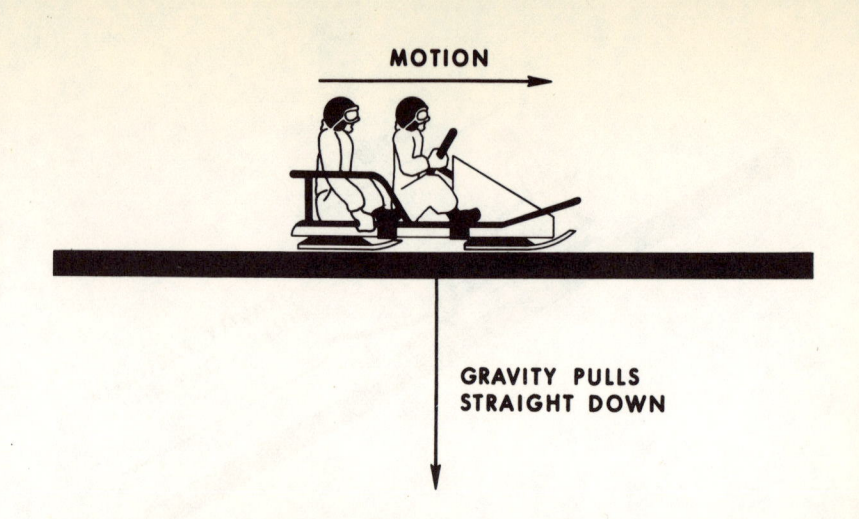

Rhonda went up a hill with a gentler slope than the one she came down. The effect of the pull of gravity therefore was not as strong on the second hill as it was on the first. She decelerated at a slower rate going up than she had accelerated coming down. As a result, she traveled a longer distance on the second hill than on the first. However, like Wes, she stopped at a height equal to the height she started from.

In a straight line forever

And now to the ride that would have led Galileo to a startling conclusion. After Edith's sled came down the hill, it traveled on level ground at constant velocity. Like

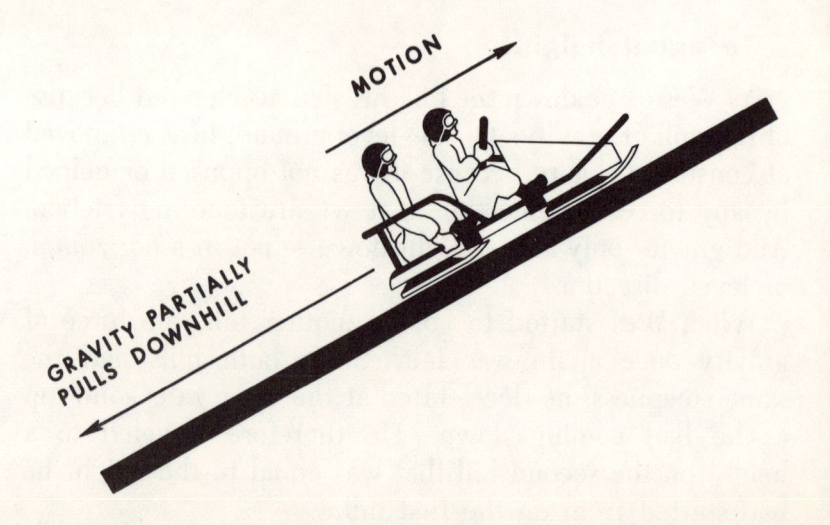

DECELERATION
Bobsled traveling uphill: The force of gravity partially pulls downhill — opposite to the motion of the sled. The sled, therefore, decelerates (decreases its velocity).

the other sleds when they were on level ground, her sled was not helped or opposed by any force. But the other sleds traveled a short distance on level ground and then went uphill. Edith's sled traveled on level ground with no forces acting on it and no hills in the way. When would it stop?

The conclusion that Galileo reached in his experiments is the same that he would have reached here: If no forces oppose the motion of a body, it will move with constant velocity forever — even without a force pushing it forward. This statement became known as the Law of Inertia.

Could Edith's sled actually coast on level ground forever? No, it could not. As Galileo would point out, the friction, or rubbing, between the sled runners and the snow would slow down the sled and eventually stop it. Galileo's thinking, however, showed the great value of imagination in science. By pretending that friction did not exist, he was the first to show that force is not needed to keep an object moving — only to slow it down, stop it, speed it up, or change its direction of motion.

The First Law

The Law of Inertia was the basis for Newton's First Law of Motion. Newton stated: "Every body continues in its state of rest, or of uniform motion in a straight line, unless it is compelled to change that state by forces impressed upon it." Thus force is needed to start a body moving, and another force is needed to stop it. Here is another way to state this law: A body at rest will remain at rest unless a force moves it. Further, a body moving at constant speed in a straight line (constant velocity) will continue its motion unless it is acted on by an outside force.

Forces can act on a body without accelerating it. In such a situation, they must balance and cancel out completely. For example, imagine that 2 horses are pulling with equal force on opposite sides of a wagon. The forces are balanced, and the wagon will remain motionless. If 1 horse pulls with greater force than the other, the forces on the wagon are unbalanced, and the wagon will move.

BALANCED FORCES
At the moment this photograph was taken, the forces on the ball (arrows) were equal and opposite — and the ball was at rest. What happened? Wilt Chamberlain (on top) increased his force and scored the point.

When he used the term "impressed" forces in the first law, Newton meant unbalanced forces. Let us look at an important force in nature — friction — that is often unbalanced. An unbalanced force of friction slows down motion because it is greater than any opposing force.

Bumps against bumps

Friction is the force that opposes motion when at least 1 of 2 bodies that are in contact moves. The surfaces of the bodies drag across each other and slow down the motion. Thus the force of friction generally acts in a direction that is opposite to the motion.

All surfaces, no matter how smooth they appear, have

some roughness. Even the surface of highly polished steel contains tiny hills and valleys that create bumps invisible to the eye. Friction results when the bumps of 1 surface hook into and catch against the bumps of another surface. Smooth surfaces produce the least friction, rough surfaces the most. You can feel this difference by dragging a finger lightly but firmly across various surfaces, such as paper, wood, a wall, and a mirror.

Friction exists between . . .

Friction is ordinarily present when bodies move anywhere on Earth. It exists between your shoes and the ground, between tires and the road, between birds in flight and the air, and between swimming fish and the water. Outer space is the only environment that is relatively free of friction. Even there, however, a space satellite may encounter particles of matter that rub against it and cause minute friction.

As both Galileo and Newton pointed out, a force is necessary to stop a body in motion. Frictional forces are normally present to do so. If a car travels at constant velocity, the force generated by the engine must also be constant to overcome friction. The force of friction is thus balanced by the force of the engine.

INVISIBLE ROUGH SPOTS THAT CAUSE FRICTION
To the naked eye, this piece of steel has a smooth, gleaming surface, much like that of a mirror. In this view, however, it is magnified 1,000 times under a microscope. The surface appears as it actually is: full of hills and valleys and all types of irregular edges.

ROAD GRIPPER
Deep treads and steel studs increase the friction between this tire and the slippery snow. As a result, the car generally starts, moves, and stops with less skidding than a car with regular tires.

77

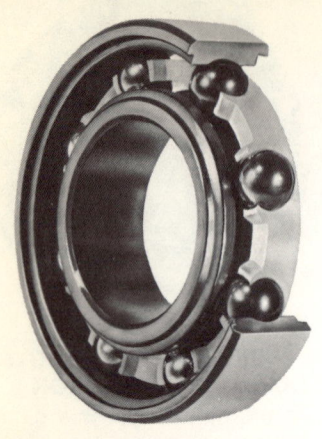

LESS FRICTION
Ball bearings reduce the friction that opposes motion. They are used in machinery and in wheels of all types. Rolling motion produces less friction than dragging or sliding motion.

Let us assume that the car is not subjected to friction. That is, friction does not exist between the tires and the road, between the body of the car and the air, and between the wheels and the axles. In addition, let us assume that air resistance does not exist. What would happen if the car's engine were shut off under these conditions? The car would roll along forever at constant velocity unless another force stopped it.

Reducing friction — and increasing it

Friction slows down motion and also causes wear between surfaces that rub together. When a large frictional force exists, there are 3 general ways to reduce it:

▶ Polish the surfaces so that they are smooth and slide over one another with less drag.
▶ Place a lubricant — a slippery substance like oil or grease — between the surfaces. The lubricant coats the surfaces and allows them to slide over one another more easily.

▶ Insert wheels, roller bearings, or ball bearings between the surfaces so that they roll over one another instead of sliding.

However, we do not always want to reduce friction. Often we want to increase it. When frictional forces are small, it is difficult to start, to stop moving, or to change direction. Running on a wet street to get out of the rain, stopping a car on an icy road, walking across a waxed floor, climbing a smooth rock, and the quick starts, stops, and turns in sports are situations in which more friction usually would be beneficial. Can you think of others?

Gravity changes the path

We have seen how the ever-present force of friction affects motion. Now let us examine how gravity and inertia — also ever-present on the Earth's surface — act together and affect motion.

Toss a coin. Squirt a watergun. Bounce a ball. Leap across a puddle. In each instance, the same thing happens. You overcome the inertia of rest of the coin, the water in the gun, the ball, and yourself. After they have started to move, all of these bodies possess inertia of motion.

Were it not for the unbalanced force of gravity, these bodies would remain in motion and travel off the Earth. (We are ignoring air resistance.) But the bodies stop moving. The coin hits the ground, and so does the water. The ball bounces lower and lower until it stops, and you land on the other side of the puddle.

Gravity changes the paths of the moving bodies. We know that if the coin were thrown straight up, it would fall straight down. But what is the path of bodies that are thrown horizontally? Let us take to the air to find out.

SLICK SURFACES
Smoothing the irregularities out of a surface reduces friction.

On the giant slide, the force of gravity is much greater than the opposing force of friction. The people whiz along at high speeds.

For the car, the reduced friction between the tires and the wet road is dangerous. There is not enough friction to hold the car on its turn, and it is skidding.

FISH
DROPS HERE

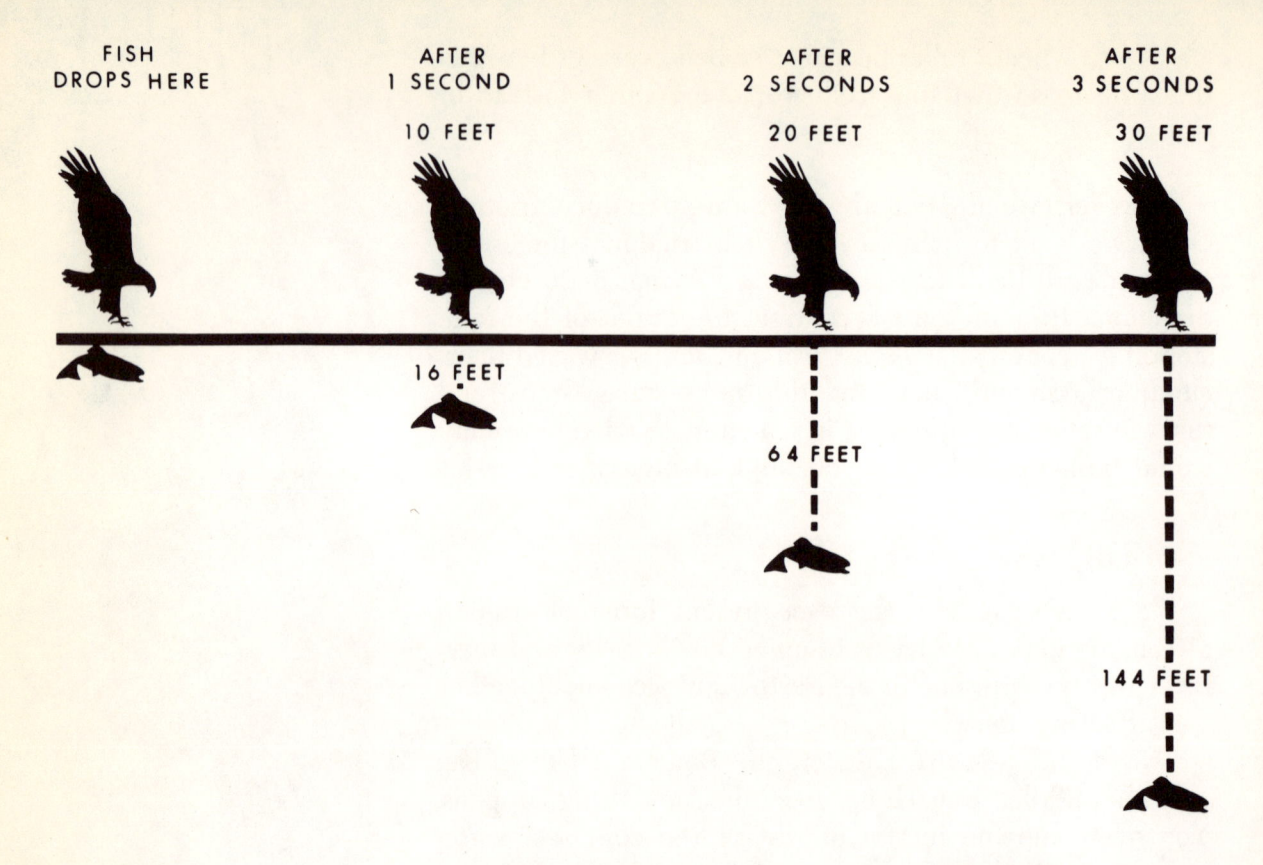

AFTER
1 SECOND
10 FEET

AFTER
2 SECONDS
20 FEET

AFTER
3 SECONDS
30 FEET

16 FEET

64 FEET

144 FEET

PARABOLIC PATH
This curve is called a parabola. Objects in motion that follow this curve or even parts of it are said to move in a parabolic path.

2 constants: velocity and acceleration

An eagle is flying over a lake and sees a large fish. It dives down, catches the fish in its claws, and soars high into the air. The eagle is flying horizontally at 10 feet per second. Suddenly, the fish wriggles free of the eagle's grasp and begins to fall back into the lake.

While falling, the fish maintains its horizontal velocity — 10 feet per second — because of inertia. Both the eagle and the fish travel the same horizontal distance in the same time, with the fish remaining directly below the eagle. Let us ignore air resistance. Then no force reduces the fish's forward inertia — until it hits the water.

During each second, the fish moves forward a constant distance — 10 feet. But the distance it falls increases in each second because of the constant acceleration of gravity (32 feet per second per second). After 1 second, the fish has moved forward 10 feet and fallen 16 feet. After 2 seconds, it has moved forward a total of 20 feet and fallen a total of 64 feet. After 3 seconds, it has moved forward a total of 30 feet and fallen a total of 144 feet.

80

We can summarize the fish's motion this way: It is moving forward at constant velocity. At the same time, it is falling at constant acceleration.

Forward and downward create a parabola

When a body falls freely (like the fish) with a motion that is not straight down, it moves in a path called a parabola. This path is actually made up of 2 motions — forward and downward. Because of inertia, the body moves forward just as if it were not falling. And it falls just as if it were not moving forward.

Only bodies that move through the air under their own power, such as birds and planes, can overcome the attraction of gravity and maintain a straight forward motion. All bodies that fall freely, however — whether they are baseballs, frogs, or jets of water — follow the same general curve. If you observe freely falling bodies, you can learn to easily recognize this curve. It may be long, short, flat, or high — but it is always a parabola.

RELATED MOTIONS
What do these moving bodies all have in common — a leaping frog, flying sparks, a bouncing ball, and a stream of water? The answer appears at the end of the index.

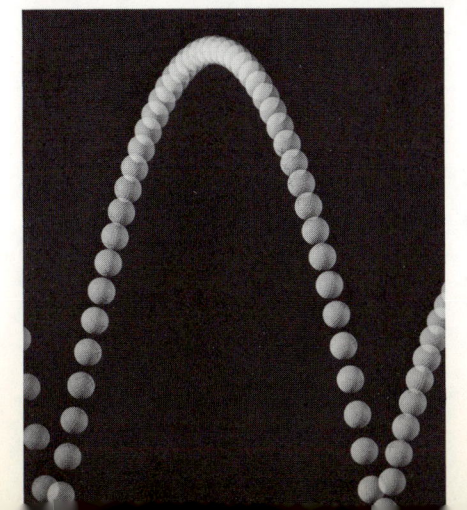

Chapter 7
MOMENTUM

Imagine that you are walking in a field when suddenly you see a large turtle crawling towards you at about ¼ mile/hour. Deciding to avoid it, you climb over a fence only to find that you are facing a young bull of the same mass as the turtle. It is charging at you at about 15 miles/hour. You have to choose between stopping the bull or climbing back over the fence and stopping the turtle. What is your decision? Why?

"A quantity of motion"

Let us consider some other impact situations. An oceanliner, traveling at 5 miles/hour, collides with a wooden dock. A baseball hits a catcher's mitt at 65 miles/hour. The oceanliner hits the dock much harder than the baseball hits the mitt. The catcher's hand stings slightly, but the wooden dock is damaged by the liner. On the other hand, a rowboat traveling at the same velocity as the liner, hits the dock and hardly dents it.

Why do these moving bodies collide with different effects? Can mass explain the difference? The turtle

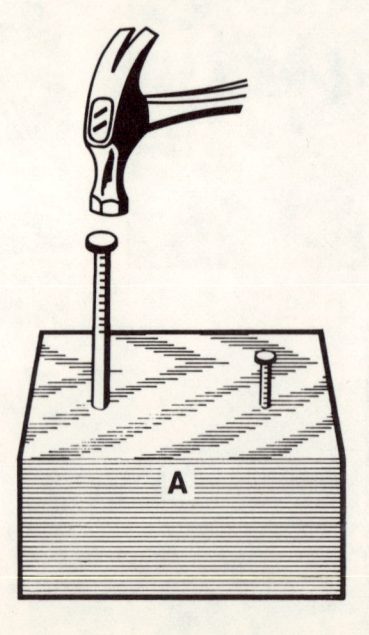

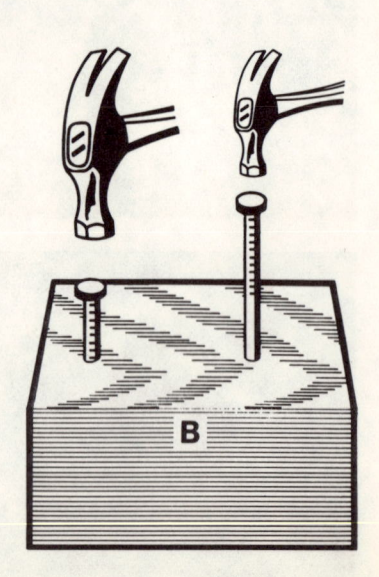

VELOCITY AND MASS DRIVE THE NAILS DEEP
In drawing A, the right nail was hit at a faster velocity than the left nail. In drawing B, both nails were hit at the same velocity. However, the hammer on the left has more mass than the hammer on the right.

LONGER TO STOP
The car and truck are traveling at the same velocity and are alongside each other on the road. Both brake at the same time. The car stops at A, but the truck cannot stop as quickly. Its larger mass carries it on to B.

and the bull have the same mass. But the bull, with its higher velocity, is the more dangerous of the two. In this instance, the high velocity accounts for the greater danger.

However, mass rather than velocity accounts for the damage caused by the oceanliner's collision with the wooden dock. Both the oceanliner and the rowboat had the same velocity. But the rowboat had no effect on the dock.

Our 2 sets of examples indicate that we are dealing with a property of motion that we have not discussed before. Both mass and velocity affect this property, which Isaac Newton described as "a quantity of motion." Today we use the term *momentum*. The more momentum a moving body possesses, the harder it is to stop.

Momentum = mass × velocity

Newton observed that momentum increases as either mass or velocity increases — or as both increase. Momentum is measured by multiplying the mass of a moving body by its velocity, which can be written

$$\text{momentum} = \text{mass} \times \text{velocity}$$

Suppose we determine the momenta of some moving bodies. (*Momenta* is the plural of momentum.) The units that measure mass and momentum are complicated, and we will not use them here. However, we do want to see how momentum is related to mass and velocity. This relationship becomes clear if we use pure numbers (without units) to describe mass and momentum. Recall that we adopted a similar approach in chapter 5 to describe force.

Like force and velocity, momentum is a vector. Remember that a vector has both size and direction. The

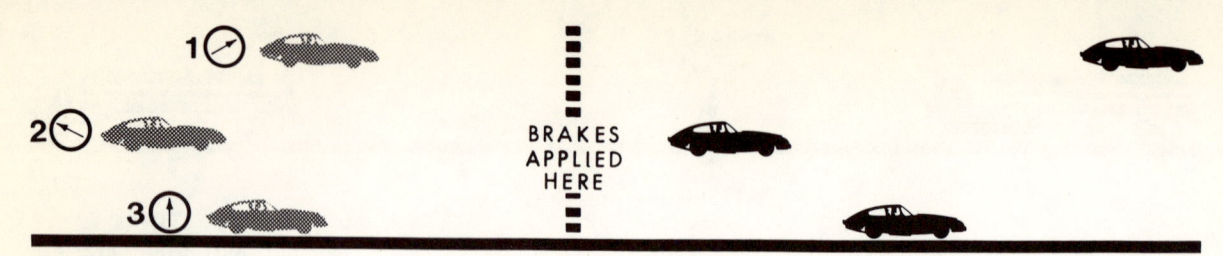

WHICH CAR IS THE FASTEST?

All 3 cars have the same mass but different velocities. Each brakes at the same time. Which car has the highest velocity? The lowest? In between? A ruler will help you find the answers, which appear at the end of the index.

direction of the momentum is the direction of the velocity of the moving body. The direction may be stated — for example, 10 momentum units, north. If direction is not important for a particular problem, however, it may be conveniently omitted, as we have done with force and velocity.

Bull or turtle?

What is the momentum of an object that has a mass of 10 units and is moving with a velocity of 15 feet per second?

mass	×	velocity	=	momentum
10	×	15	=	150 momentum units

We would obtain the same value of 150 units for momentum if the mass were 50 units and the velocity were 3 feet per second. This would also be true if the mass were

SMALL LOSS OF MOMENTUM

The playing card resists the forward motion of the bullet — but not by much. The force of resistance is very small, and it acts for a very short time. The momentum of the bullet, therefore, is reduced by only a tiny amount.

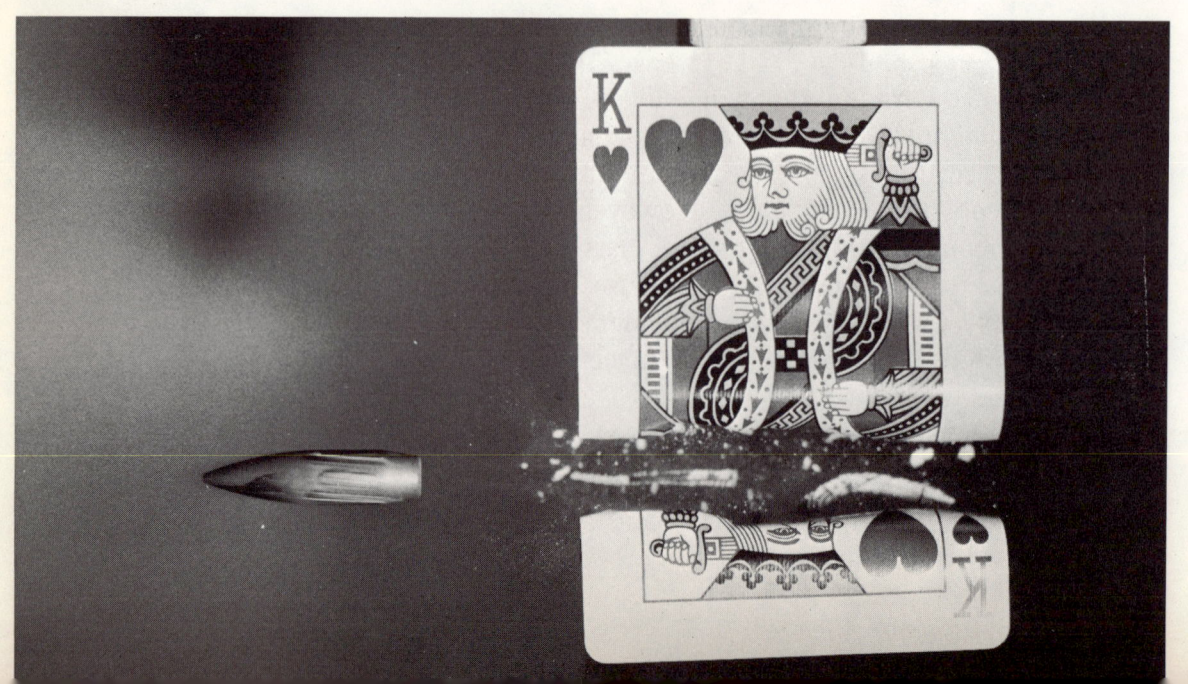

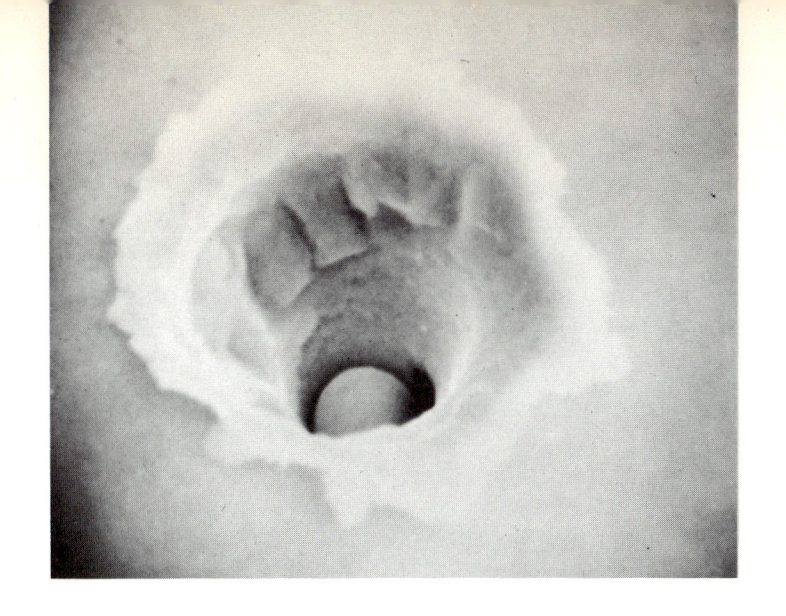

PENETRATING MOTION
Scientists are studying how rockets may be damaged by collisions with particles in space. Such particles are often extremely tiny, like the test steel pellet in the photograph. It weighs only 1 millionth of 1 billionth of 1 ounce.

The pellet is shot at an aluminum plate at 11,000 miles/hour. This high velocity gives the light pellet sufficient momentum to penetrate the aluminum. The particle and the crater it makes in the aluminum are magnified 10,000 times in this photograph.

5 units and the velocity were 30 feet per second.

Now let us see why the charging bull is more to be feared than the crawling turtle, even though both have the same mass — say, 500 units. The velocity of the bull is 15 miles/hour, that of the turtle ¼ mile/hour.

	mass	×	velocity	=	momentum
BULL	500	×	15	=	7,500 momentum units
TURTLE	500	×	¼	=	125 momentum units

The momentum of the bull is 7,500/125, or 60, times greater than the momentum of the turtle.

Equally difficult to stop

A horse of a given mass, say 600 units, is walking at 5 feet/second (about 3.4 miles/hour). A swordfish with a mass 1/12 that of the horse can swim at a speed of about 60 feet/second (about 40 miles/hour). How do their momenta compare?

	mass	×	velocity	=	momentum
HORSE	600	×	5	=	3,000 momentum units
SWORDFISH	50	×	60	=	3,000 momentum units

The horse and the swordfish have the same momentum, which means that they are equally difficult to stop. If the same opposing force is applied to each, it will take the same amount of time for each to stop. On the other hand, if both were to stop suddenly by crashing into an obstruction, they would exert the same force on the obstruction — and on themselves. Swordfish have been known to drive their swords deep into the wooden hulls of ships.

Impulse

We have seen that an object gains momentum when a force accelerates it. The amount of momentum gained depends on the size of the force and the length of time that it is applied. A small force pushing on an object for a long time can produce the same momentum as a large force acting for a short time.

Similarly, an object can be stopped — and lose its momentum — if a large force acts on it quickly or a small force acts on it for a longer time.

A force that is applied over an interval of time produces an *impulse*. This can be written

$$\text{impulse} = \text{force} \times \text{time}$$

HURRICANE MISSILE
A 200 miles/hour hurricane wind gave this 10-foot board enormous momentum, driving it through the center of a palm tree.

EXTRA MOMENTUM
The bowler takes a long swing before sending the ball down the alley. His force therefore acts for a relatively long time — applying a large impulse to the ball. The impulse provides the ball with a sizable momentum.

In our example, the same impulse was required to give the horse and the fish the same momentum. Also, the same impulse would be necessary to stop each — that is, to change the momentum of each to zero. Impulse changes momentum by either decreasing or increasing it.

Different combinations of force and time

A bat hitting a ball, a ship docking, a tomato falling on the ground, 2 cars colliding, a rocket thrusting against a spacecraft, and a door being opened all produce impulses. In each example, different forces are applied for different intervals of time to bring about changes in momentum.

Different combinations of force and time can produce the same impulse. Consider a force of 50 pounds applied for 2 seconds. As with momentum, we will bypass the units for impulse because they are complicated and unnecessary for making comparisons.

$$\text{force} \times \text{time} = \text{impulse}$$
$$50 \times 2 = 100 \text{ impulse units}$$

The same impulse is produced when a force of 10 pounds is applied for 10 seconds; 100 pounds for 1 second; and 200 pounds for ½ second. How much greater than this impulse is the impulse produced when 3 men exert a total force of 400 pounds on a piano for 30 seconds? The answer appears at the end of the index.

IMPORTANCE OF TIME
Objects move when a big enough force acts on them and overcomes their inertia. The time that the force acts is as important as the size of the force. These photographs show that the forces act long enough to drive the balls fast and far.

GREAT MOMENTUM
The arrow receives the greatest impulse when the bowstring is drawn back as far as it will go. From this position, the force is maximum. It will act on the arrow for the longest possible time — giving it great momentum.

87

SHOCK ABSORBER
The firemen lower the net as the jumper falls into it. They stretch the time of the impulse and reduce its force.

Reducing momentum

An experienced baseball player catches a ball by drawing his arms back as the ball enters the glove. A player who is new to the game, however, often holds his arms out stiffly. He will feel a large force through his glove because the momentum of the ball changes rapidly.

The experienced player cushions the shock of the ball striking his glove. By drawing his arms back, he reduces the momentum of the ball over a greater period of time. The force he feels is far less than the force felt by the new player. However, the impulse on both players' hands is the same.

The change in momentum of both balls is also the same. Both started with the same momentum because we can assume that both had the same mass and the same velocity. And they ended with zero momentum after they stopped moving.

The floor pushed back

What happens when 2 bodies of different size collide? They obviously exert forces on one another. Are these forces equal? Or does the larger body exert a greater force on the smaller body?

88

What happens when you stand on a floor? Your weight presses down on it. What does the floor do to you?

What happens when you try to drive a nail into a wall using a small board instead of a hammer? You will find small dents in the board wherever it struck the head of the nail. Why?

What happens when you tie a rope to a post and then pull on it. Does the rope pull on you? Perhaps it does not seem to do so because you do not move. Now put on a pair of roller skates, and pull on the rope again. Yank hard! This time, you will find yourself moving towards the post. Why?

Let us examine the answers to these questions and see how they are related:

▶ The 2 bodies of different size exerted equal forces on one another when they collided.

POW!
The karate expert breaks the tiles faster than most people cut butter. His arm has great velocity and therefore great momentum. The force of the resulting impulse is large enough to split the tiles.

▶ The floor pushed back at you with a force equal to your weight.
▶ The nail exerted as much force on the board as the board exerted on it. The force was large enough to dent the board.
▶ The rope pulled on you — and its pull was as great as yours.

Every applied force, as we are beginning to see, creates a force that reacts against it.

The Third Law

Your finger bleeds just the same if you stick it with a pin or stick the pin with your finger. The pin exerts a force on your finger equal to the force exerted by your finger on the pin. Both forces are exerted in the opposite direction. Newton put it this way:

"Whatever draws or presses on another is as much drawn or pressed by it. If you press on a stone with your finger, the finger is also pressed by the stone. If a horse draws a stone tied to a rope, the horse . . . will be equally drawn back towards the stone."

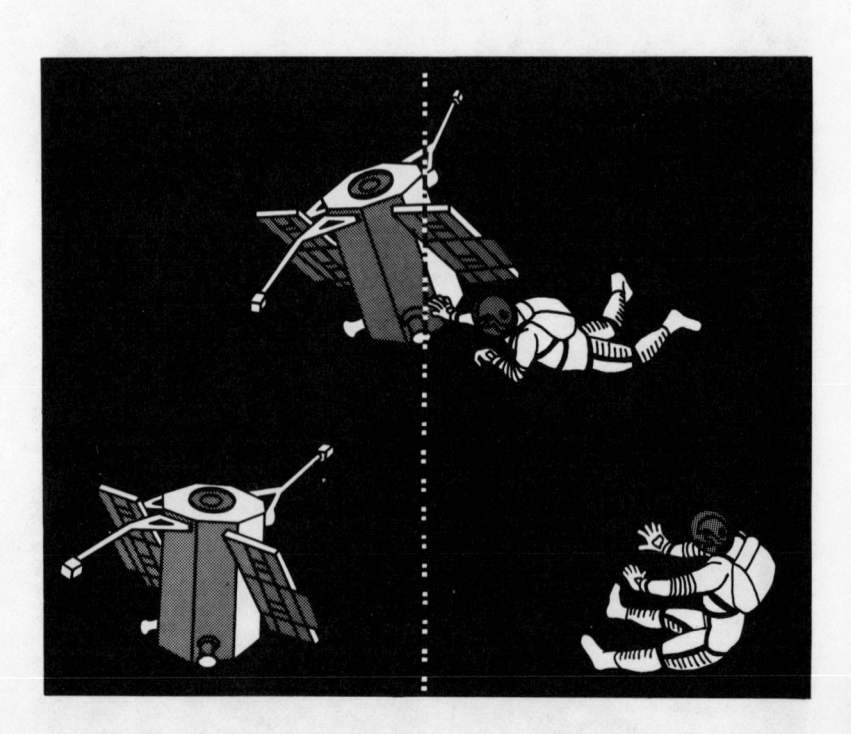

EQUAL FORCES
After checking the observation satellite, the astronaut pushes it away. The satellite pushes him in the opposite direction. Both pushes (forces) are equal in size.

Newton summarized this observation with what is now called the Third Law of Motion: To every action, there is an equal and opposite reaction. *Action* means the force exerted by 1 body on a second body. *Reaction* means the equal and opposite force exerted by the second body on the first.

Reaction on your shoes

Can an action ever occur without a reaction? No exception to the third law has ever been observed. Frogs leaping, football players colliding, and airplane propellers rotating all undergo action and reaction. Do you know how a propeller works? The propeller pushes air backward, and the plane is pushed forward by the equal and opposite reaction of the air.

EQUAL AND OPPOSITE FORCES
Both cars were traveling at the same speed. The car on the right weighs almost twice as much as the car on the left. When they crashed, the cars exerted equal forces on each other. Why?

WATER PUSHES BACK
The water is pushed out of the hose with great force. It pushes back on the hose with equal force. The hose would fly back if it were not held down by the firemen.

91

**YOU GIVE
THE EARTH MOMENTUM**
Friction is produced by the rough surfaces of the shoe and ground catching together. The shoe surface pushes back on the ground (action). The ground surface reacts by pushing forward. Result: The walker moves forward.

Does it seem strange that you walk forward by pushing backward? Try it — and feel in which direction the soles of your feet are pushing. Your feet transfer momentum to the ground, but it is too small to appreciably move the Earth.

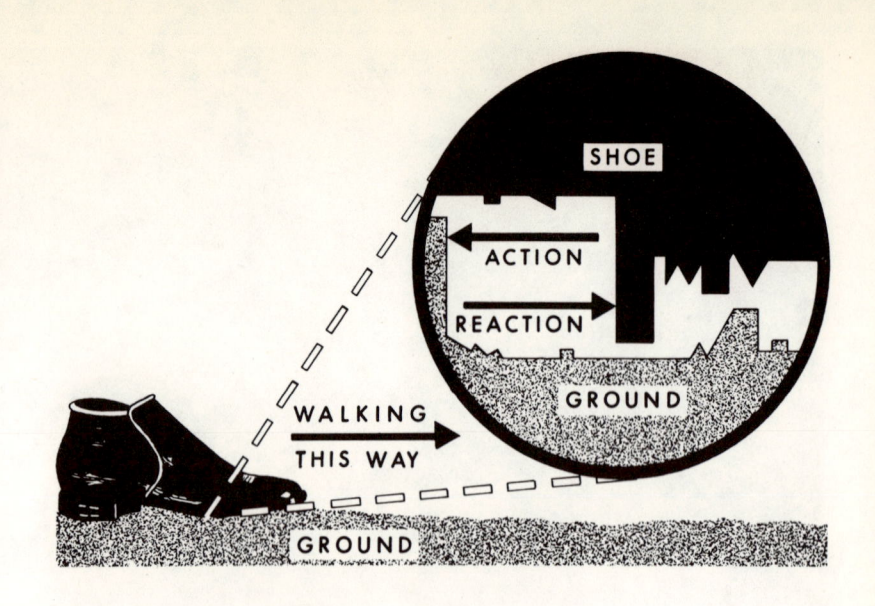

Walking is the most familiar example of action and reaction. You push backward on the ground when you walk. The ground pushes forward on you — propelling you straight ahead. The friction between your shoes and the ground (see drawing) makes it possible for you to exert an action force. Friction also makes it possible for the ground to exert a reaction on your shoes. But there are ways that motion can be produced without friction — for example, by reaction engines, which also depend on Newton's Third Law.

Reaction engines

Consider a body that exerts a large action force. The equally large reaction force will accelerate the body in the direction of the reaction. Jets and rockets work on this principle.

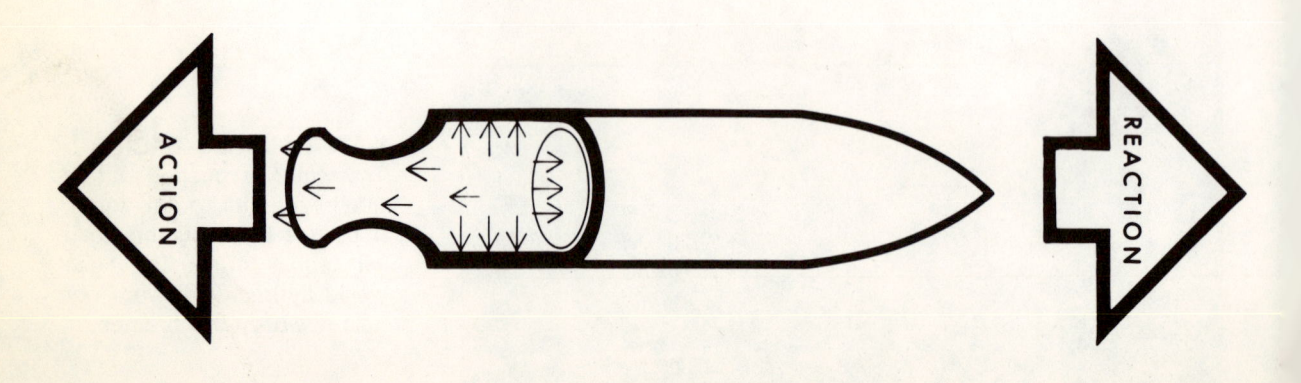

Fuel is burned and changed into gases in the combustion chamber of a rocket (or jet) engine. The gases, pushed by their own pressure, stream out of an opening at the tail end of the rocket. As they are pushed out (action), they push back (reaction) in the opposite direction. The result is that the rocket moves forward.

The gas has a much smaller mass than the rocket. Its velocity, therefore, is enormous — often about 100,000 miles/hour — so that it can impart a large velocity to the rocket. The first manned rocket to the moon, *Apollo 11*, reached a velocity of about 25,000 miles/hour.

If friction did not exist, we would have to rely on reaction engines, like rockets, to get around. For without friction, we would only be able to jump straight up. Do you know why?

Action and reaction are everywhere

Athletes who swim, high dive, and high jump all exert large action forces. They rely on equally large reaction

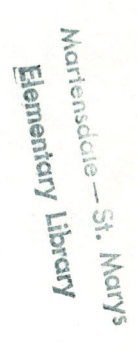

UP, UP, AND AWAY
The rocket engine on the man's back provides the force that sends him into the air. Such devices may be useful in exploring the Moon — and perhaps some day other planets.

**FULL SWING
FOR MOMENTUM**

The golfer starts his swing at 1 (the number is near the club head). He continues to 2 and 3 and hits the ball between 3 and 4.

Why does he start his swing so far back? He gains extra momentum and is able to drive the ball a great distance. This extra momentum carries his swing through 4, 5, and past 6.

forces to carry them as fast and as far as possible. The pole vault and running broad jump require the momentum gained by a running start. This momentum added to the final spring in the air produces a longer leap than is possible from a standing start. Without the momentum of a running start, a pole vaulter could hardly get off the ground. One high school broad jumper, who has won several contests, is able to jump over 23 feet from a running start. From a standing start, however, the farthest he can jump is 8 feet.

Athletes are often quite aware of the principles of momentum and action and reaction. Many of us, however, use these same principles in daily activities without thinking about them, for example:

Running before jumping over a puddle. Leaning 1 hand against a wall while opening a heavy door to prevent being pulled forward. Reaching back before swinging a hammer. Taking a running start before getting on a bicycle. Bracing against a wall before pushing a heavy piece of furniture. How many more examples can you think of?

Where does momentum go?

We have learned that a body with large momentum will create a strong impact if it collides with another body.

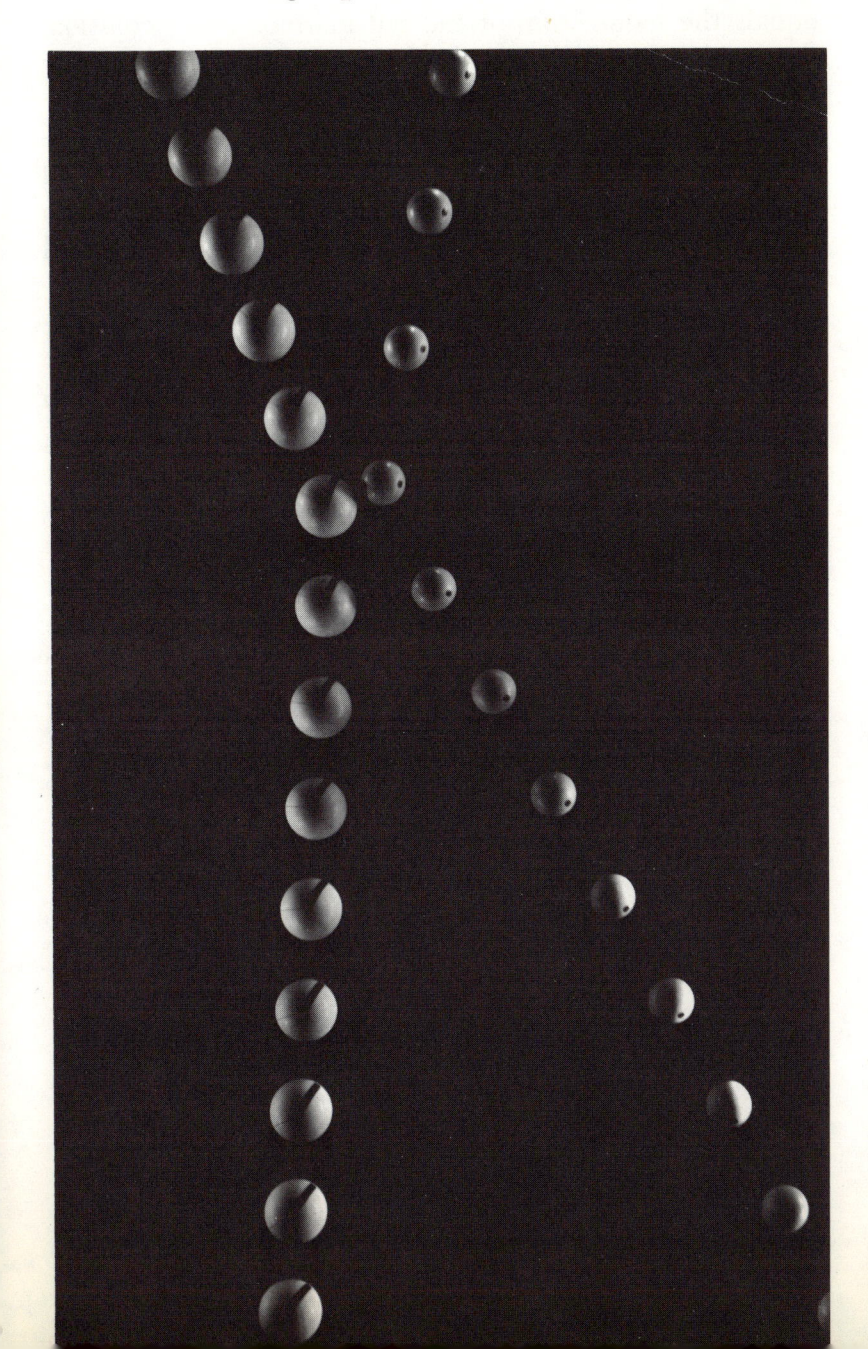

CONSERVATION OF MOMENTUM
The 2 moving balls have different masses and different velocities. They roll in from the top of the photograph, collide, and continue to roll. The sum of their momenta after collision equals the sum of their momenta before collision.

But what happens to momentum after collision? Does it just disappear? Or does any — or all — of it transfer from one body to another? To find out, let us look at 2 marbles that are going to collide.

A red marble rolling east at 2 feet/second is aimed straight at a green marble of equal mass that is at rest. Plink! The red marble stops, and the green marble rolls away at 2 feet/second, east.

The total momentum of both marbles can be found by adding the 2 momenta. Before collision, the red marble has a given momentum, and the green marble has zero momentum. Thus the total momentum before collision equals the momentum of the red marble. After collision, the total momentum equals the momentum of the body now moving — the green marble.

Both marbles have the same mass and velocity. The total momentum after collision, therefore, is exactly equal to the total momentum before collision. Total momentum is neither lost nor gained. It is, however, transferred from 1 marble to the other.

Suppose both marbles are in motion before and after they collide. In this instance, momentum is partly transferred from 1 marble to the other. Of course, the marbles may have different masses and different velocities — and, therefore, different momenta. And they may collide at an angle rather than head on.

No matter how collisions take place, the Law of Conservation of Momentum applies: When 2 or more bodies collide, the total momentum after collision equals the total momentum before collision. This law is one of the most important in science. It tells us that momentum cannot be created or destroyed but may be transferred.

TOUGH EGG?
The Third Law of Motion states: To every action there is an equal and opposite reaction. Do you think the action of the hammer could produce this unusual reaction? Or is the photographer egging us on?

Chapter 8
ROUND AND ROUND

Why does the Moon or a man-made satellite move in an orbit? What keeps the Moon from flying off into space or from plunging into the Earth? For that matter, why does the Earth revolve (follow an orbit) around the Sun? An *orbit* is the path taken by one body as it moves around another. This path may be a circle, but more often it is an oval shape called an *ellipse*. The rocket in the drawing on this page has an elliptical orbit. We will learn more about orbits as the "round and round" story of this chapter develops.

IN AND OUT OF ORBIT
At launch (A), an unbalanced reaction force accelerates the satellite. When the second stage of the rocket is ignited (B), the resulting force produces another acceleration. This causes a change in both direction and speed.

Reverse rockets cause a deceleration (C), and the satellite parachutes to Earth. How do Newton's Second and Third Laws apply to the motion of the satellite?

A change in direction

The First Law of Motion tells us that a body in motion tends to move at constant velocity (constant speed in a straight line) unless it is disturbed by an unbalanced force. However, if a body travels at constant speed in a circular path, it does not have constant velocity. Its direction continuously changes — that is, it accelerates.

Where there is acceleration, there is force. A force must be exerted to pull or push a moving body out of its straight-line path into a circular path.

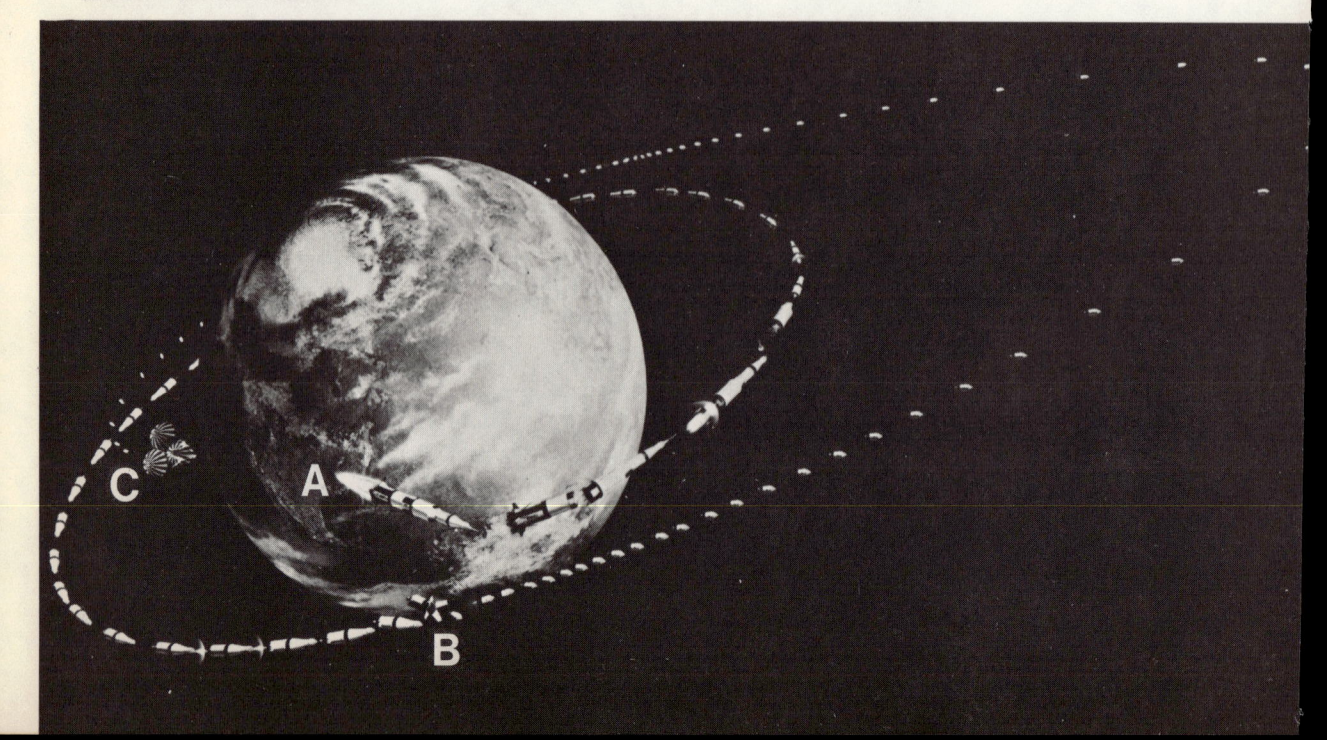

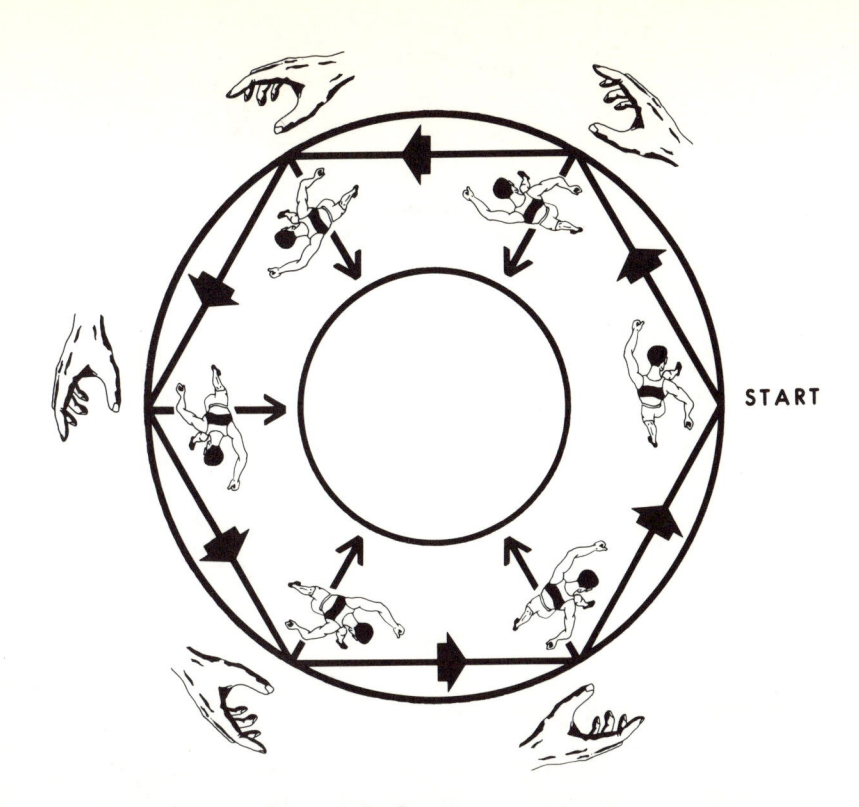

STRAIGHT LINES AROUND A CIRCLE

Each path you take is straight. However, your overall path — guided by helping hands — takes you around a circle. What happens to your path as the number of helping hands increases? See the next drawing.

Experiment in a circle

You are the subject of an imaginary experiment. We want to determine how a force must act to move you in a circular path. You are going to run in a circular path without making any effort to follow its curve. Thus you will run in a straight line. If you fail to turn, will you run into the outside rail of the track? Ordinarily, yes, but not in this experiment.

Ready, set — off you go in a straight line. As you are about to hit the rail, an assistant, who is standing outside the track, offers a helping hand. He pushes you towards the center of the track. Your direction changes. You follow the new direction in a straight line until you are about to hit the rail again, this time farther down the track. Another assistant pushes you towards the center of the track. You continue in a new direction along another straight line.

In this manner, helped by assistants, you run around the track in a path that is a series of straight lines. Your trip is made possible by forces that change your direction at just the right moment. These forces are all directed towards the center of the track.

ALMOST A CIRCLE
As the number of helping hands increases, your path becomes more and more circular. How can your path become a true circle?

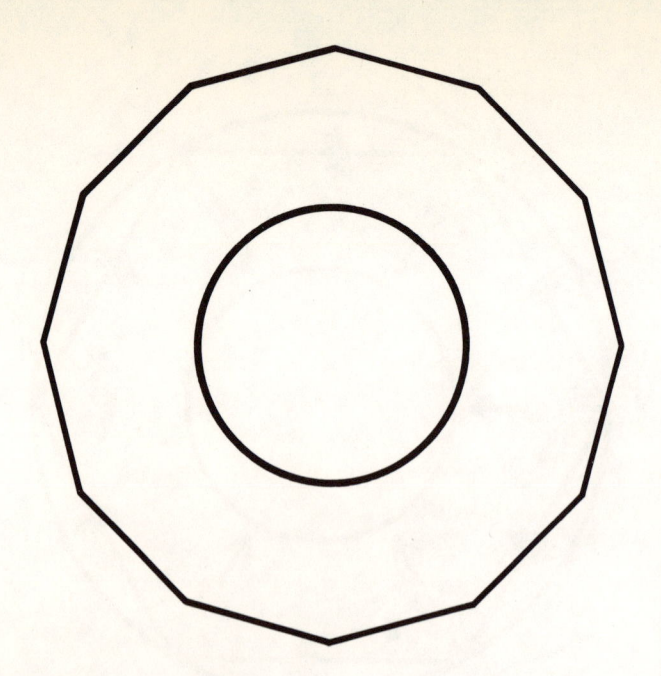

A continuous pull

When you went around the track, as the drawing shows, you had 6 assistants. Now imagine that you have 12 assistants. Your path will be more circular. As the number of forces that push you towards the center of the track increases, your path will become increasingly circular. What would happen if a force continuously pushed or pulled you towards the center of the track?

To find the answer, off you go again. But this time a force is present that pulls on you continuously. In the center of the track is a pole with a long rope tied to it. The free end of the rope is looped around your waist. As you try to run in a straight line, the rope keeps pulling you towards the center of the track. Your direction changes continuously, and you run in a circle.

Centripetal force

All circular motion occurs because a force constantly pushes or pulls a moving body towards the center of the circle. This center-seeking force is called *centripetal force*. Since a body moving in a circular path changes direction, it accelerates. A centripetal force, therefore, produces a centripetal acceleration — directed towards the center of the circle.

If you whirl a ball at the end of a string — just as you whirled at the end of the rope — the string will pull the ball into a circular path. But what of an artificial satellite or the Moon? Gravity acts like the string — and pulls the satellite and the Moon into orbits. In the same way, the Sun's pull creates orbits for the Earth and the other planets.

Keep in mind that Newton's Third Law applies everywhere — across the vastness of space as well as to a hammer hitting a nail. Thus we cannot stop with saying that the satellite and the Moon are pulled towards the Earth. In the same breath, we should observe that both bodies pull back on the Earth with equal and opposite forces. Similarly, all of the planets — pulled by the Sun — exert equal and opposite forces on it.

Centrifugal force

Let us look at what happens to a body moving in a curved path. As you round a curve in a car, you may slide on the seat and press against the door. This happens because the friction between your body and the car seat is not large enough to hold you as the car enters the curve. Your inertia causes you to slide along the seat in the direction you were moving before the car began to turn.

The sliding motion brings you against the door, which holds you in. The door exerts the centripetal force necessary to prevent you from sliding out of the car in a straight path. As a result, you move with the car in a curved path.

RINGS IN ORBIT
The rings around the planet Saturn are made up of vast numbers of satellites — the size of dust particles. Saturn's gravity provides the centripetal force that keeps the rings in orbit.

STRAIGHT AHEAD
On the straight part of the road, the car and the package have the same direction. (The arrows show the direction of motion of the car and the package on the back seat.)

When the car enters the curve, it turns and changes direction. The package, however, keeps moving in a straight line in its original direction and slides along the seat.

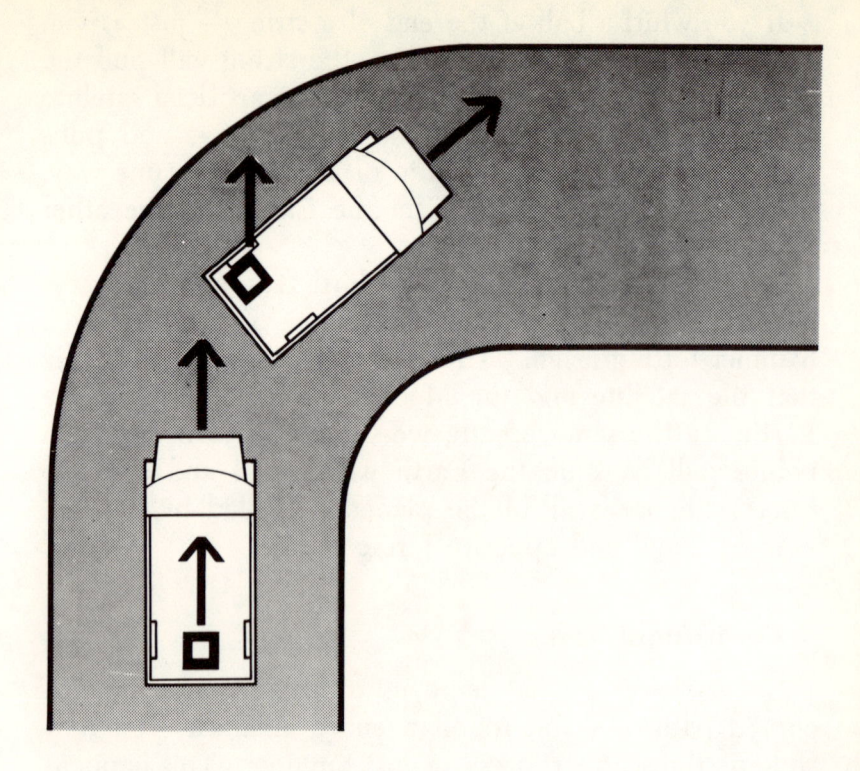

Can you see how Newton's Third Law operates here? The door pushes against you — action! Your body pushes back with an equal and opposite force on the door — reaction! This reaction to centripetal force is called *centrifugal force*.

Every force acts in a specific direction. We observed that centripetal force is center seeking — it pushes or pulls a revolving body towards the center of a circular path. Because centrifugal force is a reaction force, it acts in the opposite direction but on the other body. *Centrifugal force,* therefore, is center fleeing — it pushes or pulls away from the center of a circular path.

Faster and faster until the string breaks

Again, imagine that you are whirling a ball at the end of a string. Your hand, acting through the string, provides the centripetal force that keeps the ball in orbit. The string pulls the ball towards the center of the circle, that is, your hand. In reaction, the ball exerts an out-

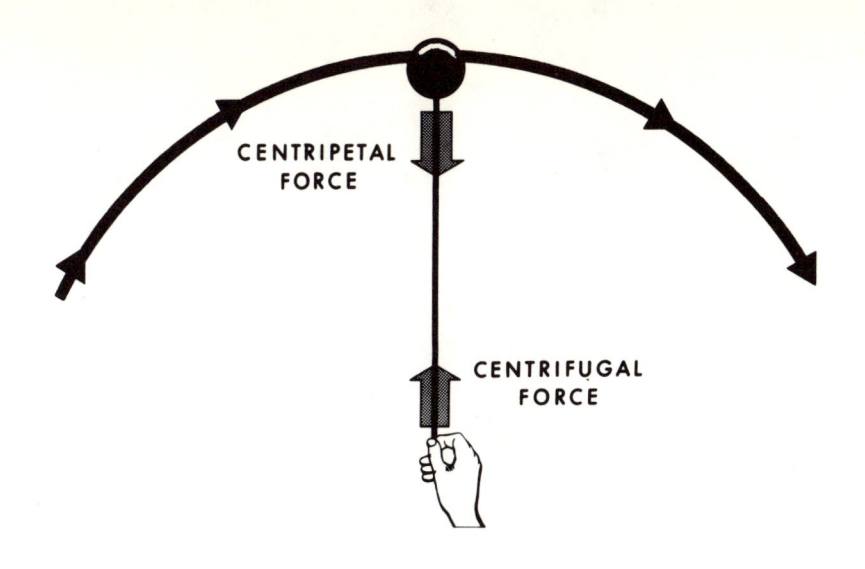

ACTION AND REACTION IN A CIRCLE
The ball is whirled around on a string. Two equal forces — centripetal and centrifugal — are present. They act in opposite directions on different objects. Centripetal force pulls inward on the ball. Centrifugal force pulls outward on the hand.

ward centrifugal force on your hand and directed away from it.

Whirl the ball faster and faster. The centripetal force will become larger and larger in order to keep the ball in orbit. As the centripetal force increases, the centrifugal force increases equally. What happens if the centripetal force required to keep the ball in orbit becomes greater than the strength of the string?

The string will break, and both forces will instantly drop to zero. What about the ball? Its inertia will carry it off at constant speed in a straight path in the direction it was moving when the string broke.

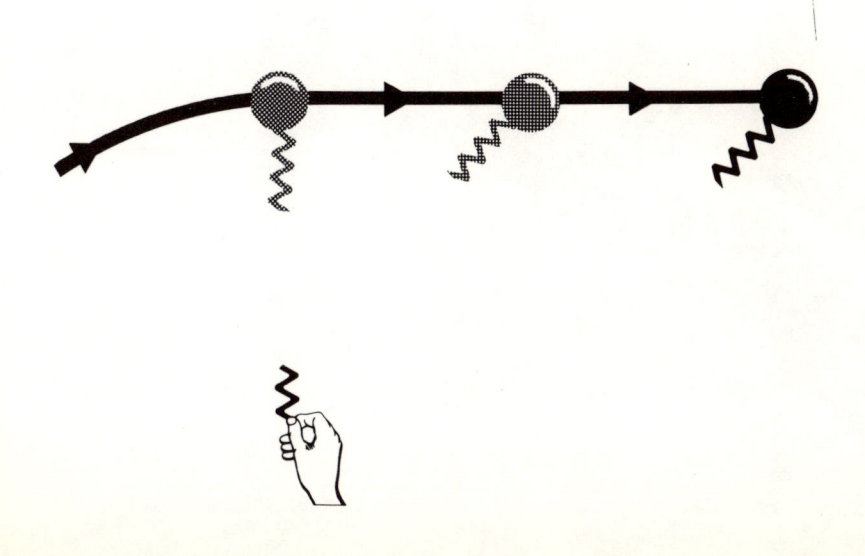

FROM CIRCULAR TO STRAIGHT MOTION
The ball shown in the previous drawing whirls around faster and faster until the string breaks. The centripetal and centrifugal forces stop immediately. So does circular motion. The inertia of the ball carries it forward in a straight line.

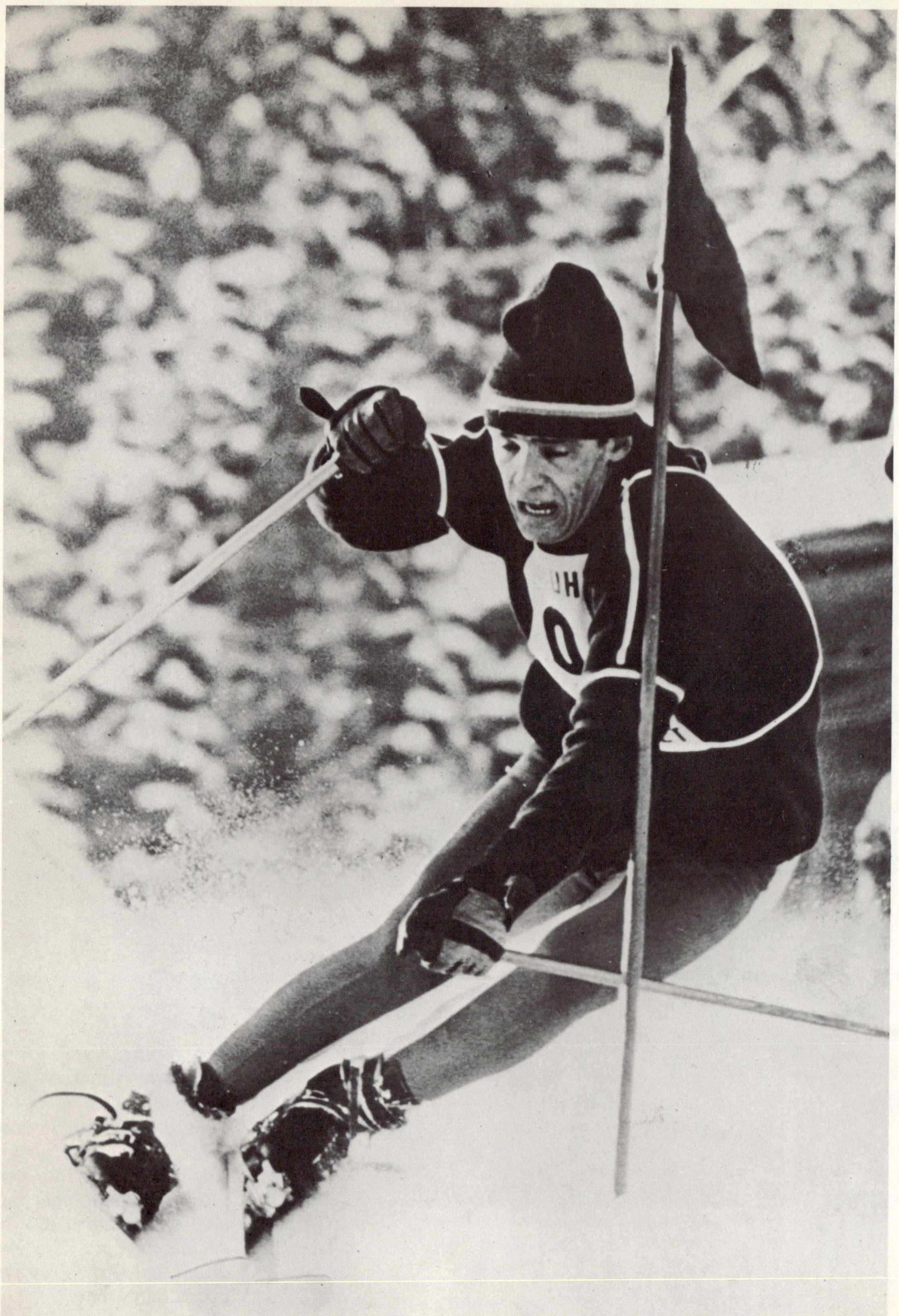

BANKING

The champion skier Jean-Claude Killy races along a curved path. His inertia tends to slide him straight off the curve. To keep from sliding to the left, he bends to the right and digs his skis into the snow.

A similar problem exists on roads. Curved sections of roads often are tilted, or banked, to prevent cars from sliding off. Bobsled runs are banked for the same purpose.

Slanted for safety

Inertia can also carry a car traveling at high speed off a curved road. When a car is traveling around a curve, frictional forces between the tires and the road exert a centripetal force on the car. The curve can be thought of as part of a circle. The centripetal force, therefore, is directed towards the center of the circle.

The high speed of the car gives it a large forward inertia. If the inertia is great enough, the centripetal force will be unable to hold the car on the curve. The car will go off the road in a straight path. For safety, many curved roads are banked. That is, they are slanted so that the outside edge of the curve is higher than the inside edge.

The slanted surface provides increased centripetal force. This force pushes inward on the car and, along with friction, helps to keep it on the curved road. Do you think there is a similarity between the centripetal force of a banked road and the force of gravity acting on a satellite?

A projectile that does not fall to the ground

We think of satellites as children of the Space Age, but they are much older than that. Some 2½ centuries ago, in a discussion of projectiles, Isaac Newton proved that satellites were possible. A *projectile* is any object that is shot or thrown forward, such as a rock, bullet, or rocket.

Picture the path of a projectile that is fired horizontally and at low speed from the top of a mountain. It will fall to the ground in a parabolic path. Now several more projectiles are fired, one at a time, horizontally. Each is ejected at a faster speed than the one before it — and, therefore, travels farther before hitting the ground. The parabolic path will become increasingly flat. Could a projectile be fired that would never fall to the ground? Newton's calculations proved that it could.

Suppose that the projectile were fired horizontally from the top of a mountain that is 100 miles high. Newton showed that the projectile would have to reach a hori-

PROJECTILE PARABOLA
The rocket blazes a fiery parabola deep into the night sky. Newton showed that projectiles, like the rocket, could go into orbit at a speed of 5 miles/second.

106

FORWARD AND FALLING

This satellite is on an imaginary trip:

Between A and B, gravity is switched off for 1 second. The satellite moves forward but does not fall.

At B, gravity is switched on again. Between B and C, inertia is switched off. The satellite falls but does not move forward.

These two motions — forward and falling — occur continuously in all orbits.

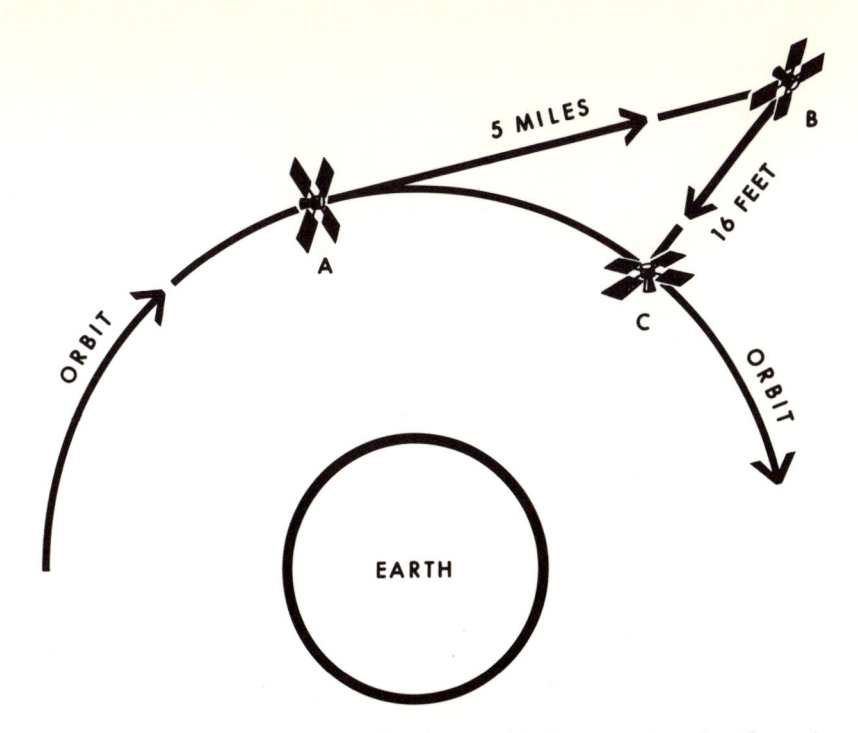

zontal velocity of 5 miles/second (18,000 miles/hour) in order to orbit the Earth. This brilliant scientist once said: "If I have seen further than other men, it is because I stood on the shoulders of giants." His vision reached far ahead into our own time, when his calculations were tested and proven correct. Satellites that now orbit the Earth at a height of about 100 miles follow a nearly circular path at the speed that Newton predicted.

Forward and downward

The forward inertia of a satellite carries it away from the Earth in a straight line. At the same time, gravitational attraction causes the satellite to fall towards Earth. The distance that the satellite travels forward is made up by the distance that it falls. Thus the satellite never gets away from Earth. The 2 motions — forward and downward — produce an orbital path around the Earth.

All orbiting bodies are falling bodies. The Moon is always falling towards the Earth, for example. And the Earth — along with all the other planets — is always falling towards the Sun. It is only the forward inertia of these heavenly bodies that keeps them from plunging into the Sun.

ELLIPSES
Unlike circles, ellipses have many shapes because some are flatter than others. Satellites are launched from Earth at different angles and speeds to obtain different elliptical orbits.

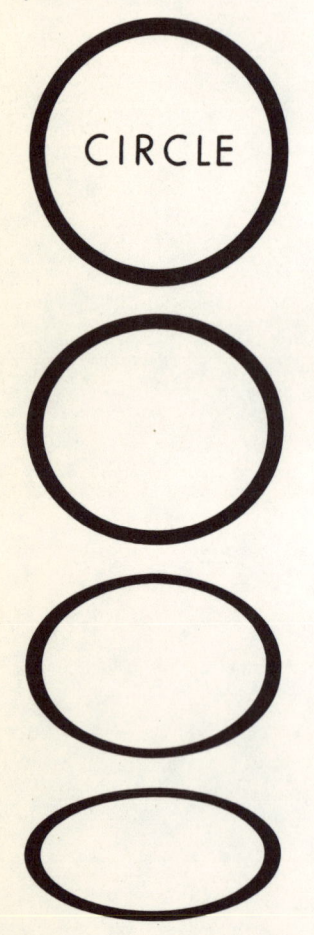

Satellite experiment

Suppose we take a closer look at the 2 motions. We will consider a satellite traveling along a circular path that rings the Earth at a height of about 100 miles. The speed of the satellite is 5 miles/second.

In our imaginary laboratory of the heavens, we have a gravity switch that allows us to shut off Earth's gravity for 1 second. During that second, the satellite will not fall. And its forward inertia will carry it ahead 5 miles.

We observe that the satellite has risen 16 feet above the circular path. Why 16? The key to the answer is 5 miles/second, the forward speed of the satellite. We have carefully selected this speed to give the satellite a 16-foot rise when the gravity switch is off for 1 second.

We pull another switch in our laboratory and shut off forward inertia. At the same time, we switch gravity on again. The satellite will drop 16 feet in 1 second and touch the circular path. That is, it will return to its original height of 100 miles. Again — why 16? This time, for the answer you may want to look at page 39, which discusses Galileo's formula for the distance traveled by a freely falling body. (The distance after 1 second is 16 feet.)

Now, at 1 second intervals, let us keep pulling first 1 switch and then the other: gravity off, forward inertia on . . . gravity on, forward inertia off . . . and so on. The satellite will travel around the Earth in a series of steps that always brings it back to the circular orbit.

Escape velocity

The advantage of our laboratory is that it allows us to control gravity and inertia. Thus we can better study and understand them. Of course, gravity and inertia do not actually stop and go. They act continuously, causing the satellite to move in a smooth curve around the Earth.

If the satellite is ejected at a speed greater than 5 miles/second, its orbit will have the shape of an ellipse. At 7 miles/second (about 25,000 miles/hour), the satellite will move forward too fast for gravity to pull it into orbit. The satellite will escape from the Earth's attraction and fly off into space. For this reason, 7 miles/second is called *escape velocity*.

Consider a body moving at high speed around a circular path. A large centripetal force must be exerted on the body to keep it on the path and prevent it from flying away. With this in mind, we can ask: Why does a satellite not remain in orbit if it speeds up and moves faster than its escape velocity? The answer is that the forward inertia of the satellite overcomes the centripetal force of Earth's gravity.

HOW FAR WILL WE TRAVEL INTO SPACE?
Even if a spaceship could move at the speed of light — 186,300 miles/second — it would take a lifetime to reach many of the nearest star systems. On a long voyage, young astronauts may return as old men. Or perhaps they will be able to hibernate while their ship speeds on.

Beyond the solar system

Spaceships now exceed the escape velocity. Astronauts have traveled to the Moon, and unmanned spaceships have probed deep into space. In the future, astronauts will ride these deep probes on long journeys that explore the solar system. By the year 2000 or sooner, they may walk on Mars.

How far beyond the solar system can man go? The answer depends on the speed of future spaceships. This speed, however, is limited. The reason is that a physical object cannot go faster than or even reach the speed of light: about 186,300 miles/second.

Man, of course, has still not achieved travel that comes close to the speed of light. At 186,300 miles/second, a beam of light could travel 7 times around the world in about 1 second. Manned space travel, as we have mentioned, has reached about 25,000 miles/hour — a speed that would carry a spaceship around the world in 1 hour.

In 1 year, light travels about 6,000,000,000,000 (6 trillion) miles. This distance, called a *light year*, is a convenient unit for measuring the almost unbelievable vastness of the heavens. We can develop a better understanding of what a light year is by comparing it to a more familiar distance: the approximately 240,000 miles that separate the Earth and the Moon. A light year is 25 million times greater than the distance between these 2 heavenly bodies (6,000,000,000,000 ÷ 240,000).

Our nearest neighboring star, Alpha Centauri, is 4.3 light years away. Thus if spaceships could travel at the speed of light, they would take 4.3 years to reach Alpha Centauri. One day space travelers may succeed in visiting a few neighboring star systems — perhaps on voyages that last a lifetime. Even such great voyages will be governed by the laws of motion that we live with here on Earth.

useful information

oranges and apples — converting units   112

table of motion conversions   114

definitions   116

recommended books   119

recommended films   120

index   121

answers to problems   123

acknowledgments   124

oranges and apples — converting units of measurement

Two scientists are trying to solve a problem. Like most work in science, their problem involves units of measurement. When the scientists finish, they discover that they have different answers.

One says, "You must have done it with oranges." The other laughs and replies, "And you sound like an apple man."

Oranges and apples? It is a humorous way of recognizing that they worked with different units of measurement. Both know that another step is necessary.

As either might say, "We won't find out if our answers agree until they are converted [changed] to the same units. You can compare oranges with oranges or apples with apples — but not oranges with apples."

One answer is 3 miles/minute, and the other is 264 feet/second. Are these answers different or do they agree? Before comparing them, we have to convert 1 answer to feet/second or the other to miles/minute. Both answers must be expressed in the same units of measurement. If we do this conversion, we will learn that the answers are equal.

To see how units are converted, let us examine what happens to a number that is multiplied by 1. The number remains the same (5 × 1 = 5). What if a number is divided by 1? Again, it is unchanged (5 ÷ 1 = 5).

Exploring further, we ask, What happens when a number is divided by itself? A fraction is created with the same numerator and denominator. Such fractions always simplify to 1 (2/2 = 1, 9/9 = 1, and 124/124 = 1). We can therefore say:

A number does not change when it is multiplied or divided by a fraction with the same numerator and denominator (6 × 4/4 = 6, and 6 ÷ 11/11 = 6).

Let us set up a slightly different type of fraction, still keeping the numerator and denominator the same. So far we have been working with pure numbers, like 4/4 and 124/124. This time the fraction will be made up of units of measurement: inches and feet.

Since 12 inches = 1 foot, the fraction 12 inches/1 foot = 1. Similarly, the fraction 1 foot/12 inches = 1. When we multiply or divide with fractions containing units, we treat the units as if they are numbers. For example, let us convert 96 inches into feet.

$$96 \;\cancel{\text{inches}} \times \frac{1 \text{ foot}}{12 \;\cancel{\text{inches}}} = 8 \text{ feet}$$

Note that the inch units cancel each other. They are crossed out just like identical numbers in the numerator and denominator of any fraction.

To convert feet into inches, we perform the same operation but reverse the fraction. For example, let us find out how many inches there are in 37 feet.

$$37 \;\cancel{\text{feet}} \times \frac{12 \text{ inches}}{1 \;\cancel{\text{foot}}} = 444 \text{ inches}$$

The English system, based on feet, pounds, and seconds, serves us for everyday measurements in the United States. These units can be divided into smaller units — for example, feet into inches. They also can be multiplied to obtain larger units — for example, pounds into tons. And they can be converted into units of the metric system.

The metric system is preferred for scientific measurements, and for everyday use in many countries. The reason is that, except for units of time, the metric system is decimal in nature. Converting 1 unit to another, therefore, is simple. It only requires multiplying or dividing by 10 or some power of 10, such as 100, 1,000, 10,000, and so on.

In both the English and metric systems, time units are expressed in seconds and larger intervals, like minutes and hours. Time units usually are not based on decimals unless they are smaller than a second.

For example, one and one-half hours is generally written 1½ hours, or 1 hour 30 minutes. But one and one-half seconds is most often written 1.5 seconds. One-tenth of a second is 0.1; one-hundredth of a second is 0.01; and three-thousandths of a second is 0.003.

The unit of length in the metric system is the meter. One meter = 100 centimeters, and 1 kilometer = 1,000 meters. The unit of mass is the kilogram. One kilogram = 1,000 grams, and 1 milligram = 1/1,000 gram, or 0.001 gram.

We can convert units within the metric system the same way we converted units within the English system. For example, let us convert a speed of 36 kilometers/hour into meters/hour.

$$36 \frac{\cancel{\text{kilometers}}}{\text{hour}} \times 1,000 \frac{\text{meters}}{\cancel{\text{kilometer}}} = 36,000 \frac{\text{meters}}{\text{hour}}$$

How can we convert 36,000 meters/hour into meters/minute?

$$36,000 \frac{\text{meters}}{\cancel{\text{hour}}} \times \frac{1 \cancel{\text{hour}}}{60 \text{ minutes}} = 600 \frac{\text{meters}}{\text{minute}}$$

We can combine both conversions into a single operation. (A number does not change in value if it continues to be multiplied or divided by 1. All of our conversion fractions = 1.)

$$36 \frac{\cancel{\text{kilometers}}}{\cancel{\text{hour}}} \times 1,000 \frac{\text{meters}}{\cancel{\text{kilometer}}} \times \frac{1 \cancel{\text{hour}}}{60 \text{ minutes}} = 600 \frac{\text{meters}}{\text{minute}}$$

Can we multiply or divide by fractions that = 1 to go back and forth between the English and metric systems?

The answer is yes. However, we need to know how the 2 systems are related. For instance, we can solve the following problem if we know that 2.2 pounds, in the English system = 1.0 kilograms, in the metric system.

Two boys who are pen pals decide to have a weight-lifting contest. One lives in Detroit, USA, and the other in Milan, Italy. The Detroit boy writes that he lifted 43.0 pounds. His friend in Milan writes back that he lifted 19.0 kilograms. Which boy lifted the heavier weight?

$$19.0 \cancel{\text{kilograms}} \times \frac{2.2 \text{ pounds}}{1.0 \cancel{\text{kilograms}}} = 41.8 \text{ pounds}$$

The winner, by 1.2 pounds, was the boy in Detroit (43.0 − 41.8).

When scientists convert many units, they often work directly from conversion tables similar to the table on the next page. A conversion table eliminates 1 or more steps in multiplication or division.

The numbers in the table should not be memorized. They serve as a reference, which means they contain information that can be looked up any time.

The table has been prepared for the study of motion. It will help you convert units for solving problems that are raised by this book and elsewhere. And it is easy to use.

Say that you want to convert 7.5 feet/second into meters/minute. Look up feet/second in the first column, and match it with meters/minute in the second column. Multiply 7.5 by the number in the third column (18.29), and the answers will be in meters/minute.

$$7.5 \times 18.29 = 137.18 \frac{\text{meters}}{\text{minute}}$$

113

How To Convert Measurement Units
That Are Useful In The Study Of Motion

Converting units of measurement is explained on pages 112 and 113.

TO CONVERT FROM	INTO	MULTIPLY BY
centimeters	feet	0.0328
centimeters	inches	0.393
centimeters	kilometers	0.00001
centimeters	meters	0.01
centimeters	millimeters	10.0
centimeters/second	feet/minute	1.968
centimeters/second	feet/second	0.0328
centimeters/second	kilometers/hour	0.036
centimeters/second	meters/minute	0.6
centimeters/second	miles/hour	0.0223
centimeters/second	miles/minute	0.000372
centimeters/second/second	feet/second/second	0.0328
centimeters/second/second	meters/second/second	0.01
days	seconds	86,400.0
feet	centimeters	30.48
feet	kilometers	0.0003048
feet	meters	0.3048
feet	miles	0.000189
feet/minute	centimeters/second	0.51
feet/minute	feet/second	0.167
feet/minute	kilometers/hour	0.0183
feet/minute	meters/minute	0.3048
feet/minute	miles/hour	0.0113
feet/second	centimeters/second	30.48
feet/second	kilometers/hour	1.097
feet/second	meters/minute	18.29
feet/second	miles/hour	0.682
feet/second	miles/minute	0.0113
feet/second/second	centimeters/second/second	30.48
feet/second/second	meters/second/second	0.3048
feet/second/second	miles/hour/second	0.682
grams	kilograms	0.001
grams	milligrams	1,000.0
grams	ounces	0.0353
grams	pounds	0.0022
inches	centimeters	2.54
inches	meters	0.0254
kilograms	grams	1,000.0
kilograms	pounds	2.205
kilometers	centimeters	100,000.0
kilometers	feet	3,281.0
kilometers	inches	39,370.0
kilometers	meters	1,000.0
kilometers	miles	0.621
kilometers	millimeters	1,000,000.0
kilometers/hour	centimeters/second	27.78
kilometers/hour	feet/minute	54.67
kilometers/hour	feet/second	0.911

TO CONVERT FROM	INTO	MULTIPLY BY
kilometers/hour	meters/minute	16.67
kilometers/hour	miles/hour	0.621
kilometers/hour/second	centimeters/second/second	27.78
kilometers/hour/second	feet/second/second	0.911
kilometers/hour/second	meters/second/second	0.2778
kilometers/hour/second	miles/hour/second	0.621
light year	miles	6,000,000,000,000.0
light year	kilometers	9,500,000,000,000.0
meters	centimeters	100.0
meters	feet	3.28
meters	inches	39.37
meters	kilometers	0.001
meters	miles	0.000621
meters	millimeters	1,000.0
meters/minute	centimeters/second	1.667
meters/minute	feet/minute	3.28
meters/minute	feet/second	0.0547
meters/minute	kilometers/hour	0.06
meters/minute	miles/hour	0.0373
meters/second	feet/minute	196.8
meters/second	feet/second	3.28
meters/second	kilometers/hour	3.6
meters/second	kilometers/minute	0.06
meters/second	miles/hour	2.24
meters/second	miles/minute	0.0373
meters/second/second	centimeters/second/second	100.0
meters/second/second	feet/second/second	3.28
meters/second/second	kilometers/hour/second	3.6
meters/second/second	miles/hour/second	2.24
miles	feet	5,280.0
miles	kilometers	1.609
miles	meters	1,609.0
miles/hour	centimeters/second	44.7
miles/hour	feet/minute	88.0
miles/hour	feet/second	1.467
miles/hour	kilometers/hour	1.609
miles/hour	kilometers/minute	0.0268
miles/hour	meters/minute	26.82
miles/hour	miles/minute	0.167
miles/hour/second	feet/second/second	1.467
miles/hour/second	kilometers/hour/second	1.609
miles/hour/second	meters/second/second	0.447
miles/minute	centimeters/second	2,682.0
miles/minute	feet/second	88.0
miles/minute	kilometers/minute	1.609
miles/minute	miles/hour	60.0
milligrams	grams	0.001
millimeters	centimeters	0.1
millimeters	feet	0.00328
millimeters	inches	0.0394
pounds	grams	453.6
pounds	kilograms	0.4536
pounds	ounces	16.0
tons	kilograms	907.19
tons	pounds	2,000.0

definitions

of scientific terms in Motion

Words that may be hard to pronounce are spelled phonetically (according to sound). When these words are spoken, a syllable between two slant marks receives greater emphasis. The list below shows how certain letters in the phonetic spelling are correctly pronounced.

a = a in hat	u = u in cut
e = e in met	ee = ee in meet
uh = a in ago	oe = o in go
ay = a in day	oh = o in sort
i = i in pit	eye = ie in pie

acceleration　　　　　　　ak sel uh /ray/ shn
The rate at which the velocity of a moving body changes. Thus acceleration equals change in velocity divided by time. A moving body accelerates when either its speed or its direction changes. Compare with deceleration.

action
The force exerted by a body on another body. Compare with reaction.

average
A number that is typical of a set of numbers. It is obtained by dividing the sum of the set of numbers by the amount of individual numbers. For example, consider the velocities 7 mi/hr, 8 mi/hr, and 12 mi/hr. The average velocity equals 9 mi/hr (7 mi/hr + 8 mi/hr + 12 mi/hr ÷ 3).

axis
An imaginary line around which a body turns. An *axle,* however, is an actual rod or shaft around which a body turns.

balanced forces
Forces that act on a body without accelerating it — thus the forces cancel out each other. If both sides in a tug of war pull in opposite directions with equal force, neither side will move because the forces are balanced.

centrifugal force　　　　　sen /trif/ uh guhl
The force acting on a body moving in a curved path that is directed away from the center of the path. Centrifugal force is an equal and opposite reaction to centripetal force.

centripetal force　　　　　sen /trip/ uh tuhl
The force acting on a body moving in a curved path that is directed towards the center of the path.

circular motion
Motion in a circular path — for example, a ball whirling around at the end of a string.

circumference　　　　　　suhr /kum/ fuhr uhns
The distance around a circle.

constant
Describes a value or measurement that remains the same — for example, constant acceleration, constant velocity, and constant temperature.

deceleration　　　　　　　dee sel uh /ray/ shn
The rate at which the velocity of a moving body slows down. Acceleration can be positive (velocity increases) or negative (velocity decreases). Thus deceleration is negative acceleration.

density
Mass per unit volume of a substance. For example, the density of water is 62.4 pounds per cubic foot; of butter 59 pounds per cubic foot; of gasoline 42 pounds per cubic foot; of glass 155 pounds per cubic foot; of sugar 100 pounds per cubic foot; and of steel 490 pounds per cubic foot.

displacement
Distance along a straight line in 1 direction. It is the shortest distance between 2 points. Compare with total path.

distance
The total path (not displacement) that a moving body travels. Distance equals displacement only when distance is measured as a

straight line in 1 direction.

ellipse   i /lips/
A shape somewhat like an oval or a flattened circle.

escape velocity
The velocity required by a space vehicle to overcome the gravitational attraction of a heavenly body and fly off into space. The escape velocity on Earth is 7 miles/second. On the Moon, it is 1.5 miles/second, and on Mars, it is 3.1 miles/second.

force
Any push or pull that tends to start, stop, or alter the motion of an object. A force applied to an object tends to accelerate it.

formula
A mathematical statement that shows how different quantities are related — for example, distance = speed × time.

frame of reference
A specific location against which the motion or position of an object can be described. For example, car A is traveling at 30 miles/hour, and car B is traveling at 60 miles/hour. The frame of reference for both cars is the Earth, which is regarded as stationary. However, if we say that car B is moving 2 times faster than car A, the frame of reference for car B is car A.

free fall
The motion of a body that is only under the influence of gravity. We feel weight on Earth because the ground beneath us resists the tug of gravity. But an astronaut in a satellite feels weightless and floats. Nothing resists Earth's gravity because both he and the satellite are falling freely together.

friction
The force that opposes motion when at least 1 of 2 bodies that are in contact moves. The surfaces of the bodies drag across each other and slow down the motion.

gravity
The force of attraction between any mass and the Earth. Gravity pulls all objects towards the Earth's center. Because of gravity, falling bodies have the same acceleration: 32 feet/second/second.

impulse
The product obtained when force is multiplied by the time that the force is applied.

inclined plane
A flat surface that is sloped — for example, a hill or a tilted board.

inertia   in /ur/ shuh
The resistance of matter to a change in motion, either in speed or direction. Thus a body that is moving tends to keep moving. And a body at rest tends to remain at rest.

inverse
A number that is turned upside down. The inverse of 5 is 1/5; of 6 is 1/6; of 2/3 is 3/2; and of 3/5 is 5/3.

law
Scientific (not legal): A description of what always takes place in nature under certain conditions.

light year
The distance traveled by light in 1 year; about 6,000,000,000,000 (6 trillion) miles.

mass
Three useful definitions are: 1) A measure of the amount of matter in a body. Since the amount of matter in a body is always the same, mass never varies. 2) A measure of the amount of inertia in a body. 3) A measure of the amount of force necessary to produce an acceleration in a body.

momentum   moe /men/ tuhm
A measure of the amount of motion in a body. Momentum equals the mass of the body times its velocity. A force is required to change the momentum of a body.

motion
A continuous change of position. Motion is measured against a frame of reference.

orbit /ohr/ bit
The path taken by 1 body as it moves around another. This path may be a circle, but most often it is an ellipse.

parabola puh /rab/ uh luh
A shape somewhat like this: ⌒ When a body falls freely with a motion that is not straight down, it moves in a parabolic path. This path is made up of 2 motions — forward and downward.

per
Divided by, or each. A division line is often substituted for *per*. Thus 5 feet per second, or 5 feet in each second, may be written 5 feet/second.

projectile pruh /jek/ tuhl or pruh /jek/ teyel
Any object that is shot or thrown forward, such as a rock, bullet, or rocket.

random
Not planned or organized, without a definite pattern. To move at random is to move in any direction according to chance.

reaction ree /ak/ shn
The equal and opposite force exerted by a body when another body acts on it. Compare with action.

relative to
When compared to.

revolution
Orbital motion, that is, the movement of 1 body around another. The Earth revolves around the Sun, and the Moon revolves around the Earth. Compare with rotation.

rotation
The turning of a body, for example, the Earth, on its axis. Compare with revolution.

scalar /skay/ luhr
A measurement that shows size without direction, such as speed, length, time, and temperature. Compare with vector.

solar system /soe/ luhr
The Sun together with the 9 planets, their moons, and all the other heavenly bodies that orbit the Sun.

speed
The distance a moving body travels per unit of time. Speed equals distance divided by time — for example, 75 miles/hour.

time
A measurement of the interval between 2 given events, such as the beginning and end of an action. A *unit of time* is a single measurement of time, like 1 second, 1 minute, or 1 hour.

total path
The actual distance traveled by a moving body, including all curves and turns that may be present. Compare with displacement.

unbalanced forces
Forces that accelerate a body because they are unequal and do not cancel out each other. Compare with balanced forces.

vector /vek/ tuhr
A measurement that shows both size and direction, such as displacement, force, momentum, velocity, and acceleration. Compare with scalar.

velocity vuh /los/ uh tee
Speed in a given direction. Velocity equals displacement/time — for example, 8 feet/second, east. The velocity of an accelerating body equals acceleration multiplied by time.

vibrate /veye/ brayt
To move back and forth, like a stone swinging on the end of a string. Atoms and molecules vibrate endlessly. When a tuning fork vibrates, it produces a sound.

weight
A measurement of the force exerted by gravity on a body. The weight of a body depends on its distance from the center of the Earth. As this distance decreases, the body becomes heavier. As it increases, the body becomes lighter.

recommended books

BASEBALL-ISTICS by Robert Froman. Discusses the physics of motion with examples from baseball. Putnam, 1967. Hardcover, $3.49.

DOCTOR POSIN'S GIANTS by Dan Q. Posin. The lives and works of famous scientists, including Galileo and Newton. Harper and Row, 1961. Hardcover, $4.50.

EXPLORING AND UNDERSTANDING ROCKETS AND SATELLITES by Dan Q. Posin. Explains the nature of rocket flight and the physics behind it. Benefic Press, 1967. Hardcover, $2.60.

FASTER AND FASTER: THE STORY OF SPEED by Raymond F. Yates. Explores various aspects of speed in water, on land, and in the air. Harper and Row, 1956. Hardcover, $3.50.

HOW FAST? HOW FAR? HOW MUCH? by William Moore. Describes how speed, gravity, interplanetary distances, etc., are scientifically measured. Explains instruments used for these measurements. Putnam, 1966. Hardcover, $3.49.

MONORAILS by Derek Harvey. Describes the development of the monorail from the first in 1824 to those now in use. Putnam, 1965. Hardcover, $3.29.

MOTION by Evans Valens. Very basic account of the nature of motion. Hale, 1965. Hardcover, $3.50.

NEWTON AND GRAVITATION by Colin Ronan. Reproductions of Newton's experimental work and calculations used in arriving at his laws of motion and gravitation. Jackdaw Publications (Grossman), 1967. Kit, $2.95.

ORBIT: PICTURE STORY OF FORCE AND MOTION by Hy Ruchlis. Relates the basic laws of motion to orbital flight. Harper and Row, 1958. Hardcover, $3.95.

THE PROMISE OF SPACE by Arthur C. Clarke. A grand tour of space, including basic physics and imaginative ideas. Pyramid, 1970. Paperback, $1.25.

REALM OF MEASURE by Isaac Asimov. Historical development of systems of measurement — from feet and yards to pounds, gallons, and seconds per second. Fawcett World, 1960. Paperback, 60¢.

SST: PLANE OF TOMORROW by Lou Jacobs, Jr. The first United States supersonic transport — how it was developed and the problems involved. Golden Gate Junior Books, 1967. Hardcover, $3.95.

THE STORY OF CARS by Gwynn Morris. A detailed account of land vehicles, from the invention of the wheel to air-cushion cars. Putnam, 1963. Hardcover, $3.95.

THE STORY OF TRAINS by Mortimer Simmons. The development of the train. Putnam, 1963. Hardcover, $3.95.

YOU AND RELATIVITY by Mary L. Clark. A nonmathematical account of frames of reference and the theory of relativity. Children's Press, 1965. Hardcover, $3.00.

WINGS, LEGS, OR FINS by Henry B. Kane. Describes the motion of land, sea, and air animals. Knopf, 1965. Hardcover, $3.25.

recommended films

These films are available to teachers, librarians, and organizations interested in education. Rental rates are generally for 1 to 3 days. All films are 16 mm and have sound except where noted. Most rental films can also be purchased.

ACTION AND REACTION. Develops Newton's Third Law with demonstrations and experiments, using both familiar material and special techniques. 15 min. Color rental $10. BFA Educational Media, 11559 Santa Monica Blvd, Los Angeles, Calif 90025.

ALL ABOUT WEIGHTLESSNESS. The unique problems that face spacemen as they venture into outer space. 11 min. Color rental $6. Walt Disney Productions, 350 S Buena Vista Ave, Burbank, Calif 91503.

BALANCING FORCES. Examines the scientific principles that relate to center of gravity, inertia, and centrifugal force — applied to work, play, and transportation. 14 min. B&W rental $7. Universal Education and Visual Arts, 221 Park Ave S, New York, NY 10003

CONSTANT VELOCITY AND UNIFORM ACCELERATION. Shows how these measurements can be made, using a glider along a level track and down an inclined plane. 4 min. Silent. Super 8 mm. Color. Sale only: $24.95. Ealing Corp, 2225 Massachusetts Ave, Cambridge, Mass 02140.

FORCE OF GRAVITY. Explains the theory of gravity and its effects. 10 min. B&W rental $6.50. McGraw-Hill Textfilms, 330 W 42 St, New York, NY 10018.

FORCES. Investigates the nature of balanced forces, unbalanced forces, and impact. 14 min. Color rental $8. B&W rental $5.50. Encyclopedia Britannica Educational Corp, 425 N Michigan Ave, Chicago, Ill 60611.

GALILEO'S LAWS OF FALLING BODIES. Experiments with the inclined plane and freely falling bodies are shown through slow motion and freeze-frame photography. 6 min. B&W rental $4.50. Encyclopedia Britannica Educational Corp, 425 N Michigan Ave, Chicago, Ill 60611.

GRAVITY, WEIGHT AND WEIGHTLESSNESS. Examines the effects of gravity on satellites in orbit. 11 min. B&W rental $6.50. BFA Educational Media, 11559 Santa Monica Blvd, Los Angeles, Calif 90025.

JET AND ROCKET ENGINES. Models and animation explain the reaction principle in both jet and rocket engines. 10 min. Color rental $4.00. B&W rental $2.75. Indiana University, Audio-Visual Center, Bloomington, Indiana 47401.

LAWS OF MOTION. Studies Newton's laws of motion and events that led to their discovery. Includes experiments with moving balls and demonstrations with an automobile, locomotive, airplane, and gun. 13 min. Color rental $6.50. B&W rental $4.50. Encyclopedia Britannica Educational Corp, 425 N Michigan Ave, Chicago, Ill 60611.

MAKING THINGS MOVE. Describes forces that make things move, forces that prevent things from moving, and forces that make things difficult to move, such as gravity and friction. 11 min. Color rental $6.50. B&W rental $4.50. Encyclopedia Britannica Educational Corp, 425 N Michigan Ave, Chicago, Ill 60611.

SPACE ORBITS. Discusses how space orbits follow the natural laws discovered by Isaac Newton. 18 min. Color. Free. Dept of the Air Force, AVVUTU, Headquarters Aerospace Audio-Visual Service (MAC), Norton Air Force Base, Calif 92409.

WHAT IS UNIFORM MOTION? Investigates uniform motion, the use of force to start and stop a motion, and the role of friction in reducing motion. 14 min. Color rental $8. B&W rental $5.50. Encyclopedia Britannica Educational Corp, 425 N Michigan Ave, Chicago, Ill 60611.

index

a acceleration, 31-40
    atomic particles, 54-55
    constant acceleration, 80-81
    defined, 31
    effect of gravity on, 65-66, 72-74
    effect of slope on, 37
    inclined plane, 38-39
    Newton's Second Law, 46-48
    related to centripetal force, 100
    related to force, 42-43, 44, 47, 63, 98
    related to mass, 45-48, 61, 63
action, 91-95, 101, 102, 103
anemometer, 26-27
Aristotle, 36, 37, 65
average velocity, 31
axis, 50-51

b balanced force, 77
banked roads, 105-106
Brownian movement, 6
bubble chamber, 54-55

c centrifugal force, 50-51, 101-103
centripetal force, 100-103, 105, 106, 109
circular path, 50-51, 99-100
Conservation of Momentum, Law of, 96
constant acceleration, 80-81
constant velocity, 31, 74, 75
converting units of measurement, 22-23, 112-115

d Da Vinci, Leonardo, 58-59
deceleration, 33-34, 42, 74
density, 45
displacement, 16, 17, 18, 19
distance, 16-18, 21-22, 42-43, 67
    defined, 16
    displacement, 16, 17, 18, 19
    formula for, 21-22, 39
    related to acceleration, 39, 42-43, 46
    total path, 17-18, 19, 20
    traveled at Equator, 50-51

e ellipse, 9, 98, 108
escape velocity, 108-109

f First Law, Newton's, 75
force, 41-70
    balanced, 77
    centrifugal, 50-51, 101-103
    centripetal, 100-103, 105, 106, 109
    defined, 42
    effect of, 41-42
    equal and opposite, 91-95, 101, 102
    frictional, 76-79
    momentum, 82-96
    related to acceleration, 44, 45-48, 63, 65-66
    related to distance, 43
    related to impulse, 86-87
    related to time, 86-87
    unbalanced, 75-76
frame of reference, 10-12
free fall, 37-38, 39-40, 65, 108
friction, 75, 76-79, 92, 93, 101, 105, 106

g Galileo, 36-40, 65, 71-75
gravity, 66-70, 72-74
    defined, 63
    effect on satellites, 101, 107, 108, 109
    effect on weight, 64, 65
    gravitational attraction, formula, 67
    Newton's Universal Law of Gravitation, 69-70
    related to inertia, 79-81

i impulse, 86-87, 88, 89
inclined plane, 38-39
inertia, 71, 72, 79-81, 101, 103, 105
    banked roads, 105-106
    defined, 62
    effect on satellites, 107, 108, 109
    related to gravity, 79-81
Inertia, Law of, 75
interval, 15
inverse, 66

l Leonardo da Vinci, 58-59

m mass, 44-48, 61-66
    related to acceleration, 45-48, 61, 63
    related to gravity, 69
    related to momentum, 83
    rockets, 93

measurement, units of, 22-23, 47, 112-115
momentum, 82-96
   conservation of, 95, 96
   effect of impulse on, 86-87, 88, 89
   extra, 94
   formula for, 83
motion
   circular, 99, 100-106, 109
   defined, 13
   direction of, 18, 19, 25-27
   effect of force on, 44
   effect of friction on, 76-79
   effect of gravity on, 72-73
   effect of mass on, 44-48, 61-62
   measurement of, 14-23
   molecular, 5-6
   random, 6
   subatomic, 54-55

n Newton, Isaac, 44, 106-107
   First Law of Motion, 75
   Second Law of Motion, 46-48
   Third Law of Motion, 90-91, 92, 101, 102
   Universal Law of Gravitation, 69-70

o orbit, 98, 101, 106-107, 108

p parabola, 80, 81
parabolic path, 80, 81, 106
projectile
   atomic, 54-55
   satellite, 106-107

r reaction, 91-95, 101, 102, 103
reaction engines, 92-93
reciprocal, 66
revolution of Earth, 9, 98
rocket
   engine, 92-93
   on man's back, 93
   sled, 35-36
rotation of Earth, 9-10, 50-51

s satellite, 107-109
scalar, 29
second (unit of time), 15
Second Law, Newton's, 46-48
solar system, 9, 101, 107, 110
speed, 19-23, 28, 29
   defined, 19
   formula for, 20
   See also velocity
star motion, 15

t Third Law, Newton's, 90-91, 92, 101, 102
time, 14-16, 20, 29
   defined, 14
   effect on impulse, 86-87
   interval, 15
   measurement of, 15
   the second, 15
   unit of, 20
total path, 17-18, 19, 20

u unbalanced force, 75-76
Universal Law of Gravitation, 69-70

v vector, 18, 26, 34, 42, 83
velocity, 25-31, 93, 107
   average, 31
   compared with speed, 28
   constant, 31, 74, 75
   defined, 25
   escape, 108-109
   formula for, 26
   related to momentum, 83

w weather vane, 26-27
weight
   above the Earth, 67-68
   on other planets, 68

ANSWERS TO PROBLEMS
APPEAR ON THE NEXT PAGE.

answers to problems

page 15
The camera lens was open at least 24 hours. This is the time it takes for the Earth to make 1 full rotation — and for the camera to photograph a complete circle of the heavens.

page 17
Each has a displacement of 6.0 miles. The crow flies 6.0 miles, but the man walks 9.5 miles. The man therefore, travels 3.5 miles farther than the crow (9.5 miles − 6.0 miles = 3.5 miles)

page 21
Speed = distance/time. After 1 second, her speed is 3 feet/second. After 3 seconds, her speed is still the same (9 feet/3 seconds = 3 feet/second).

page 29
Temperature is a scalar because it has size but not direction. Weight is a vector. Ordinarily, direction is not stated when an object is weighed. However, keep in mind that weight measures the force of gravity (which has both size and direction) on the object.

page 33
Velocity = acceleration × time. After 10 seconds, the velocity of the car is 3 miles/hour/second × 10 seconds = 30 miles/hour. The car had a velocity of 40 miles/hour when it began to accelerate. The final velocity, therefore, is 70 miles/hour (30 miles/hour + 40 miles/hour).

page 40
In the formula that follows, distance is in feet, acceleration in feet/second/second, and time in seconds. Note that the acceleration of a freely falling object is 32 feet/second/second.

distance
= ½ acceleration × time × time
= ½ 32 × 1 × 1
= 16 feet (after 1 second)

The same formula is applied to solve the second part of the problem:

distance
= ½ acceleration × time × time
= ½ 32 × 3 × 3
= 144 feet (after 3 seconds)

page 64
Gravity exerts a slightly greater pull on the man at the beach. He is closer to the center of the Earth than the man on Mt. Everest.

page 68
The astronaut is 20,000 miles (16,000 miles + 4,000 miles) from the center of the Earth. Thus he is 5 times farther from the center of the Earth than he would be if he were standing on the surface (5 × 4,000 miles = 20,000 miles).

weight in space
$$= \frac{1}{\text{distance} \times \text{distance}} \times \text{weight on surface}$$
$$= \frac{1}{5 \times 5} \times 160 \text{ pounds}$$
$$= \frac{160 \text{ pounds}}{25} = 6.4 \text{ pounds}$$

page 73
"It is obvious. Gravity opposes their motion."

page 81
They all move in a parabolic path.

page 84
Car 1 has the highest velocity. Car 3 has the lowest. Car 2 is in between.

page 87
The number of men is unimportant and can be ignored when we apply the formula

impulse = force × time
= 400 × 30
= 12,000 impulse units

This impulse is 120 times greater than the impulse in the first example (12,000 impulse units/100 impulse units = 120).

123

acknowledgments

We are grateful to the following organizations and individuals for the photographs, art, and information they contributed to this book. Credits are listed by page numbers and letters (T for top, B for bottom, L for left, R for right, and C for center).

Acme Shear Co 29C
American Museum of Natural History 22, 23
Atlas Safety Equipment Co 88
Bausch & Lomb 8BR, 36
Bear Archery 87B
Belfort Instrument Co 27R
Bell Aerospace Div of Textron, Inc 57B, 93
Brookhaven National Lab 54, 55 both
Brunswick Corp 86B

Chrysler Corp 71
Consul General of Japan 56C
Davidson, T (National Audubon Soc) 81TL
Dr Pepper Co 64BR
Edgerton Harold E 15TL, 41 all, 60T, 81BL, 84B, 87T both, 94
Education Development Center 95
ESSA 27L, 86T
Federal Highway Administration 91T
Florida News Bureau 47
French Tourist Office 104
General Bearing Co 78T both
General Electric Co 29TR, back endpaper
General Motors Corp 105T
Goodyear Tire & Rubber Co 24, 77B
Hess, Felix 19
IBM Corp 58, 59T
Jenny, Hans (courtesy of IBM) front endpaper, 6B
Lick Observatory 15TR, 15BR, 101, 109
Los Alamos Photo Lab 60B
Lott, James (Scholastic Magazines — Kodak Photography Awards) 49
Mankato Free Press 64TR
Metropolitan Museum of Art, Gift of Paul Bird, Jr, 1962 59B
Missouri Tourism Commission 38
Mott, Jacolyn A 58T
Museum of Modern Art 5
NASA 30, 61 both, 85
National Bureau of Standards 79B
NY Convention & Visitors Bureau 13TL, 13BL
NY Fire Dept 81BR, 91B
NYS Dept of Commerce 105B
North American Rockwell Corp 98
Oyama, M (This Is Karate) 62, 89
Rensselaer Polytechnic Institute 57T
St Olaf College 48
San Francisco Warriors 76
Schwinn Bicycle Co 42
Science Related Materials, Inc 7T
Shurgin, Leslie 97 all
Sky-Slides International, Inc 79T
Smithsonian Astrophysical Observatory 70
Smithsonian Institution 25
Taylor Instrument (Sybron Corp) 29TL, 29BR
Texas Instruments, Inc 66 both
Triborough Bridge & Tunnel Authority 56T
Union Pacific Railroad 20, 64L
United Artists 14, 52 both, 53 all
USAF 35, 106
US Forest Service 8T, 8BL, 13TR
US Steel Corp 77T
US Track and Field Federation 28
Vapor Corp 29BL
Warner Lambert 81TR
Washington State Dept of Commerce 56B
Westinghouse Electric Corp 50
WHO 7B
Yerkes Observatory 44

124

BOOKS ON MANY SUBJECTS

We publish books for young people in the humanities and the sciences. These books are highly recommended by review and educational journals for use in libraries, schools, and homes.

The text of each book is profusely illustrated with photographs and drawings — reinforcing the reading process for young people, who are growing up in a highly graphic age.

We will be pleased to send you a complete catalog.

CREATIVE EDUCATION PRESS

Division of Creative Educational Society, Inc.
Mankato, Minnesota 56001

Machine that duplicates human motion

"There is no magic formula for achieving creativity — it is simply a way of life in a laboratory dedicated to discovery and invention."

PAUL SALZBERG

AMERICAN CHEMIST (BORN 1903)